The Court and
the Constitution

The Court and the Constitution

THE OLIVER WENDELL HOLMES LECTURES

1951

BY OWEN J. ROBERTS

KENNIKAT PRESS/PORT WASHINGTON, N. Y.

THE COURT AND THE CONSTITUTION

Copyright 1951 by The President and Fellows of Harvard College
Reissued in 1969 by Kennikat Press by arrangement with the
Harvard University Press
Library of Congress Catalog Card No: 70-86057
SBN 8046-0584-X

Manufactured by Taylor Publishing Company   Dallas, Texas

Essay and General Literature Index Reprint Series

THE OLIVER WENDELL HOLMES LECTURES

The late Justice Oliver Wendell Holmes left a legacy in his will for the Harvard Law School. By a vote of the President and Fellows of Harvard College, the income from this bequest is to be "devoted to paying the honorarium of a lecturer to be known as the Holmes Lecturer, and the expenses of publication of his lectures; this lecturer to be appointed for a series of lectures not oftener than once in three years by the Corporation upon recommendation of the Faculty of the Law School."

Contents

The Court and
the Constitution

Introduction

The framers of the Constitution were conscious that they were creating a dual form of government which had no parallel in political history. They proposed to establish a National Government separate from and superior to the constituent states in the matters committed to it, but they meant that in all matters not committed, the states were to retain the attributes of sovereignty.

Some powers both must necessarily exert. Neither could live without the power of taxation. Neither could exist without the power of regulation of individual conduct. Neither could succeed without a system of justice. In the exercise of power in each of these spheres, the national government or the state government, as the case might be, was to act on the individual citizen. Each citizen of a state would owe obedience to laws of two sovereignties, because he would be a citizen of each.

It was recognized in the Philadelphia Convention that the legislature of the nation, on the one hand, and that of the state, on the other, might transgress the area belonging to the other sovereign. Recognizing the probability of conflict between nation and states, in the exercise of power, the strong federalists in the Convention at first advocated a provision "that the National Legislature should have authority to negative all [state] laws which they should judge to be improper."[1]

[1] Madison's Notes, June 8, 19. There are so many editions of Madison's Notes that I cite them by date rather than by the page of any edition.

Many doubted the wisdom of placing such a power of veto in the Congress. Others were against it as an invasion of the states' prerogative of internal police. One suggestion was made that the power of the Supreme Court to pass upon the constitutional validity of national or state laws would be sufficient.

The latter view prevailed. In repeated resolutions it was proposed that the National Judiciary should *inter alia* have jurisdiction of questions which involve "the national peace and harmony."[2] The Convention thus abandoned any idea of veto of state laws by the national legislature and determined to commit the solution of questions which might disturb the peace and harmony of the federation to the judiciary, though the language finally used was "cases arising under" the Constitution.   Controversies arising out of the alleged transgression by one government upon the authority of the other were relegated to the Supreme Court.

In the performance of the function so conferred upon it, the Court has repeatedly found itself called upon to announce propositions nowhere expressly stated in the Constitution. It has had to formulate rules deduced from the fundamental nature of our dual system. Instances might be multiplied, but I have chosen to examine three fields in which conflicts of jurisdiction have had to be resolved, either by necessary implication from the very structure and nature of our federal system, or by constructions given to phrases in the Constitution which were thought necessarily to be implied from the grant of general powers. The three fields I want to consider are those of taxation, regulation, and due process.

[2] Madison's Notes, June 13, 16, 19, 21, July 18 and 26.

I. Sovereignty and the Power to Tax

The taxing power is one of the fundamental powers of government. Each of the states possessed it when the Constitution was framed. This instrument recognizes state power to tax and purports to limit it only in two respects. No state, except by the consent of Congress, may lay any impost or duty on imports or exports except those absolutely necessary for executing its inspection laws, or lay any duty on tonnage without the consent of Congress.[1]

As the national government was to be one of limited and express powers, it was necessary to give it the power of taxation; Article I, Section 8, clause 1, provides: "The Congress shall have power to lay and collect taxes, duties, imposts and excises . . . but all duties, imposts and excises shall be uniform throughout the United States." The only limitations on this sweeping grant of power are that no capitation or other direct tax shall be laid unless in proportion to the census and that no tax or duty shall be laid on articles exported from any state.[2]

It is thus plain that substantially the entire field of taxation remains open to each of the governments, national and state, and that the burden of taxation of each sovereign may fall on the same persons, natural or artificial, the same property, privilege, or activity.

[1] Article I, § 10, clauses 2 and 3.
[2] Article I, § 9, clauses 4 and 5.

There was no thought that Congress might lay taxes upon the member states or that the states might levy a tax upon the nation. What of taxes on the property of a sovereign? There is no instance of an effort by the federal government to levy a tax on the property of a state. One reason this is so is that such a tax would be a direct one, which the federal government could not levy without apportionment. The requirement of such apportionment has deterred the imposition of direct federal taxes. But the states have essayed to tax federally owned property. In several instances the Supreme Court has been called upon to rule on efforts to collect such taxes. It has uniformly and categorically denied the power of a state to lay taxes on lands owned by the federal government, whether public lands in the western domain or smaller tracts otherwise acquired by the United States.[3]

The theory behind this ruling is obviously that it is inconsistent with sovereignty that one sovereign's property be taxed by another. It is a concept about which there has been no dubiety.

It was not long after the creation of the national government that a difficult problem of statesmanship came to the Court in *McCulloch* v. *Maryland*.[4] This was the problem of taxability of agencies or instrumentalities of government. The Congress chartered the United States Bank, of which the United States became a stockholder. A branch office was established in Baltimore. The operations of the bank were believed to be detrimental to those of similar state institutions. The Maryland legislature enacted a law, levying a tax on the operation of issuing notes by any corporation not licensed so to do by Maryland. The tax was to be paid by using for such notes paper stamped by the state. The rate was high. As

[3] McGoon v. Scales, 9 Wall. 23 (1869); Van Brocklin v. Tennessee, 117 U.S. 151 (1886); New Brunswick v. United States, 276 U.S. 547 (1928).
[4] 4 Wheat. 316 (1819).

an alternative to the use of stamped paper, the bank might pay a lump sum of $15,000 per annum. As the Bank of the United States was not licensed by Maryland, its operations fell within the statute. The state asserted the tax and attempted to penalize an officer of the bank for failure to pay it.

The Maryland court sustained the act and gave judgment for the state. Appeal was taken to the Supreme Court. There the judgment was reversed and the state tax held invalid as applied to the bank.

Three matters were decided: First, that Congress may implement the powers expressly conferred on it, by creating appropriate agencies or means or instrumentalities for the purpose. This would be so, in the absence of the conferred power to make all laws "necessary and proper" for carrying into execution the granted powers. The decision on this point seems not open to question, and never since has been questioned.

Secondly, though no express authority is given to incorporate a national bank, such an institution is well adapted to aid in the promotion of the fiscal powers of the federal government, and Congress, therefore, has power to create such a corporation for these ends. Again, the proposition has never been questioned. The system of national banks finds its justification in the principle.

Thirdly, the bank was an instrumentality of the United States, created to exercise its sovereign powers, and the tax in question being a tax on its operations ran afoul of the Constitution. This is the holding that has given great trouble in its later application.

Chief Justice Marshall stated propositions which have repeatedly been quoted in later decisions and have become the warp of the law on the subject of the exercise of the taxing power of nation and state. He said:

"In America, the powers of sovereignty are divided between

the government of the Union, and those of the States. They are each sovereign, with respect to the objects committed to it, and neither sovereign with respect to the objects committed to the other."

We shall see that this phrase needs explication in the light of later decisions.

"There is no express provision for the case, but the claim has been sustained on a principle which so entirely pervades the constitution, is so intermixed with the materials which compose it, so interwoven with its web, so blended with its texture, as to be incapable of being separated from it, without rending it into shreds."

Here is an avowal that the Court is not construing the words of the Constitution, but enforcing the principles on which it rests.

"If we measure the power of taxation residing in a State, by the extent of sovereignty which the people of a single State possess, and can confer on its government, we have an intelligible standard, applicable to every case to which the power may be applied. We have a principle which leaves the power of taxing the people and property of a State unimpaired; which leaves to a State the command of all its resources, and which places beyond its reach, all those powers which are conferred by the people of the United States on the government of the Union, and all those means which are given for the purpose of carrying those powers into execution. We have a principle which is safe for the States, and safe for the Union. We are relieved, as we ought to be, from clashing sovereignty; from interfering powers; from a repugnancy between a right in one government to pull down, what there is an acknowledged right in another to build up; from the incompatibility of a right in one government to destroy, what there is a right in another to preserve. We are not driven to the perplexing inquiry, so unfit for the judicial department, what degree of taxation is the legitimate use, and what degree may amount to the abuse of the power. The attempt to use it on the means employed by the government of the Union, in pursuance of the constitution, is itself an abuse, because it is the usurpation of a power which the people of a single State cannot give.

"We find, then, on just theory, a total failure of this original right to tax the means employed by the government of the Union, for the execution of its powers. The right never existed, and the question whether it has been surrendered, cannot arise.

. . . . .

"That the power to tax involves the power to destroy; that the power to destroy may defeat and render useless the power to create; that there is a plain repugnance, in conferring on one government a power to control the constitutional measures of another, which other, with respect to those very measures, is declared to be supreme over that which exerts the control, are propositions not to be denied. But all inconsistencies are to be reconciled by the magic of the word *confidence*. Taxation, it is said, does not necessarily and unavoidably destroy. To carry it to the excess of destruction would be an abuse, to presume which, would banish that confidence which is essential to all government.

"But is this a case of confidence? Would the people of any one State trust those of another with a power to control the most insignificant operations of their State governments? We know they would not. Why, then, should we suppose that the people of any one State should be willing to trust those of another with a power to control the operations of a government to which they have confided their most important and most valuable interests?"

I shall have more to say of this.

"If the States may tax one instrument, employed by the government in the execution of its powers, they may tax any and every other instrument. They may tax the mail; they may tax the mint; they may tax patent rights; they may tax the papers of the custom-house; they may tax judicial process; they may tax all the means employed by the government, to an excess which would defeat all the ends of government. This was not intended by the American people. They did not design to make their government dependent on the States."

This purports to define the scope of the immunity. As we shall see, grave difficulties have arisen in its application.

"This opinion does not deprive the States of any resources which they originally possessed. It does not extend to a tax paid by the real property of the bank, in common with the other real property within the State, nor to a tax imposed on the interest which the citizens of Maryland may hold in this institution, in common with other property of the same description throughout the State. But this is a tax on the operations of the bank, and is, consequently, a tax on the operation of an instrument employed by the government of the Union to carry its powers into execution. Such a tax must be unconstitutional."

Again, we shall find the definition of operations of a government or its agencies or instrumentalities has given trouble.

These things seem clear from the opinion: It is the Court's function to preserve the federal system by striking down such exercise of the taxing power by either sovereign as will hamper, impede, or destroy the other. The touchstone is not the extent of the burden, but the total lack of power to impose it, however slight. Nor is the purpose of the tax important. A clear case of hostile discrimination against the federal agency in favor of state institutions could have been made out in *McCulloch* v. *Maryland*, but counsel and Court passed this and went to the fundamental issue of power.

This case was the forerunner of a series of some eighty cases of major importance dealing with state taxation of federal activities and federal taxation of state activities. In no field of federal jurisprudence has there been greater variation and uncertainty. About one quarter of these decisions have been expressly or tacitly overruled, modified, or ignored in later cases. Doubtless the explanation is that the Court has been called upon to exercise statesmanship in an uncharted region rather than interpretation of the text of the instrument; to implement policy rather than law.

The holding of *McCulloch* v. *Maryland* that the state was without power to collect the tax is founded in the view that if a tax is lawful a court is incompetent to set any limit to the extent or the effect of the levy. Perhaps no expression of the great Chief Justice has been more often quoted than this: "The power to tax involves the power to destroy." For over a century the phrase was repeated and used as the criterion of decision in this field.

In *Veazie Bank* v. *Fenno*[5] it was said: "The power to tax may be exercised oppressively upon persons, but the responsibility of the legislature is not to the courts, but to the people by whom its members are elected."

McCray v. *United States*[6] sustained a federal tax on colored oleomargarine which was obviously intended to reach into the states and to drive that commodity, a competitor of butter, out of existence. The Court refused to consider the motive or the effect of the law as affecting its validity, or the fact that a similar result could not have been effected by an exercise of the commerce power.

[5] 8 Wall. 533, 548 (1869).
[6] 195 U.S. 27 (1904).

In *Flint* v. *Stone Tracy Co.*,[7] this was said of a federal corporate excise tax in respect of its effect:

"It is urged that this power can be so exercised by Congress as to practically destroy the right of the states to create corporations, and for that reason it ought not to be sustained, and reference is made to the declaration of Chief Justice Marshall in *McCulloch* v. *Maryland* that the power to tax involves the power to destroy. This argument has not been infrequently addressed to this Court with respect to the exercise of the powers of Congress."

Of such contention the Court said in *Knowlton* v. *Moore*:[8]

"This principle is pertinent only when there is no power to tax a particular subject, and has no relation to a case where such right exists. In other words, the power to destroy, which may be the consequence of taxation, is a reason why the right to tax should be confined to subjects which may be lawfully embraced therein, even although it happens that in some particular instance no great harm may be caused by the exercise of the taxing authority as to a subject which is beyond its scope. But this reasoning has no application to a lawful tax, for if it had, there would be an end of all taxation; that is to say, if a lawful tax can be defeated because the power which is manifested by its imposition may when further exercised be destructive, it would follow that every lawful tax would become unlawful, and therefore no taxation whatever could be levied."

Quoting from *McCray* v. *United States*:[9]

"No instance is afforded from the foundation of the government where an act which was within a power conferred, was declared to be repugnant to the Constitution, because it appeared to the judicial mind that the particular exertion of constitutional power was either unwise or unjust.

[7] 220 U.S. 107, 168 (1911).

[8] 178 U.S. 41 (1900).

[9] *Supra*, note 6.

. . . . .

"Since, as pointed out in all the decisions referred to, the taxing power conferred by the Constitution knows no limits except those expressly stated in that instrument, it must follow, if a tax be within the lawful power, the exertion of that power may not be judicially restrained because of the results to arise from its exercise."

In *Magnano Co. v. Hamilton*,[10] the Court observed: "From the beginning of our government, the courts have sustained taxes although imposed with the collateral intent of effecting ulterior ends which, considered apart, were beyond the constitutional power of the lawmakers to realize by legislation directly addressed to their accomplishment."

And at the present term in *United States v. Sanchez*,[11] a tax avowedly intended to regulate and control the use of a harmful drug was sustained.

The Supreme Court has never hinted, much less decided, that a tax can be voided because it is excessive in amount.

More than a century after *McCulloch v. Maryland*, Marshall's phrase was quoted and relied on in *Panhandle Oil Co. v. Knox*[12] in striking down a state sales tax imposed on sales of gasoline to the United States. In dissenting Mr. Justice Holmes said:

"It seems to me that the state court was right. I should say plainly right, but for the effect of certain dicta of Chief Justice Marshall which culminated in or rather were founded upon his often quoted proposition that the power to tax is the power to destroy. In those days it was not recognized as it is today that most of the distinctions of the law are distinctions of degree. If the states had any power it was assumed that they had all power, and that the necessary alternative

[10] 292 U.S. 40, 47 (1934).   [12] 277 U.S. 218 (1928).
[11] 340 U.S. 42 (1950).

was to deny it altogether. But this court which so often has defeated the attempt to tax in certain ways can defeat an attempt to discriminate or otherwise go too far without wholly abolishing the power to tax. The power to tax is not the power to destroy while this court sits. The power to fix rates is the power to destroy if unlimited, but this court while it endeavors to prevent confiscation does not prevent the fixing of rates."[13]

This statement was made by one who had concurred in the decisions in the *McCray* and *Flint* cases and who wrote the opinion in *Gillespie v. Oklahoma*[14] setting aside a state tax on the net income of a lessee from the United States of Indian lands for production of minerals, so far as the base of the tax included income traceable to operations on the leased land. In that case, Mr. Justice Holmes quoted with approval this language from the opinion in *Indian Territory Ill. Oil Co. v. Oklahoma:*[15] "A tax upon the leases is a tax upon the power to make them, and could be used to destroy the power to make them."

In a recent case the Holmes dissent in the *Panhandle* case is cited, but without any application to the facts involved.[16]

I am bound to say I do not understand the later view of Mr. Justice Holmes. Can he mean that the one sovereign is free to tax the instrumentalities of the other up to the point where

[13] The analogy is not sound. The confiscation cases rest on the prohibition against the uncompensated taking of private property for public use of the Fifth Amendment, applied to the states, as has been held, by the Fourteenth. The basis is that to require a privately owned public service company to serve, without the right to abandon the service, for rates so low as to eat into its capital is a taking of that capital without compensation. No other basis has, to my knowledge, been suggested. What is fair or just compensation is the very issue. Taxation, on the other hand, is a taking without compensation to the taxpayer, for the uses of government, of organized society collectively.

[14] 257 U.S. 501 (1922).

[15] 240 U.S. 522, 530 (1916).

[16] Oklahoma Tax Comm. v. Texas Co., 336 U.S. 342 (1949).

nine justices or a majority of them pragmatically declare the burden has become, in their opinion, too heavy? This could only mean that the Court is a super-legislature.

The Court has struggled with unsatisfactory results to apply the test Marshall laid down—that power is lacking in a state by taxation to retard, impede, burden, or in any manner control the operations of laws constitutionally enacted by Congress. This formula seems to leave open for decision by the Court in specific cases the issues of the legality of the creation and function of the instrumentality, of the quality of the instrumentality, and of the impact of the tax.

It was early held that so-called stock of the United States, or bonds or notes issued by it, were proper means of exercise of the fiscal powers of the nation and that their status as such precluded state taxation of them.[17] Certificates of indebtedness issued to contractors for goods furnished were so classified.[18] Patents have been included.[19] Officers and employees of government departments have been held means and agencies for executing federal laws.[20] Contracts are means of such execution. For many years lessees of mineral resources of the federal government who were to pay royalties based on production were held to be agencies or instrumentalities of the government in considering their status for state taxation.[21]

We inquire what has been held a forbidden burden upon such federal means and instrumentalities. In *Weston* v. *Charleston*,[22] the Court held that a local tax on intangibles levied on a taxpayer who owned United States stock could

---

[17] Weston v. Charleston, 2 Pet. 449 (1829); Bank of Commerce v. New York City, 2 Black 620 (1863); Bank Tax Case, 2 Wall. 200 (1864); Bank v. Supervisors, 7 Wall. 26 (1868).

[18] The Banks v. The Mayor, 7 Wall. 16 (1868).

[19] Long v. Rockwood, 277 U.S. 142 (1928); overruled in Fox Film Corp. v. Doyal, 286 U.S. 123 (1932).

[20] Dobbins v. Commissioners, 16 Pet. 435 (1842).

[21] See, *e.g.*, Gillespie v. Oklahoma, 257 U.S. 501 (1922).

[22] *Supra*, note 17.

not be imposed in respect of that stock. The theory was that to permit the levy would adversely affect, in some measure, the government's power to borrow, for, with this tax, it would obtain less advantageous terms than would be the case were the securities tax exempt.

Since that decision the invariable rule has been that an ad valorem tax on federal securities in the hands of the taxpayer is a forbidden burden on federal activity.[23] With less reason, it seems, the same ruling was extended to certificates of indebtedness.[24]

The question of the directness of the tax burden arose in *Home Insurance Co. v. New York*.[25] There the state imposed on a corporation chartered by it a tax styled a franchise tax, measured by a percentage of capital stock plus dividends. The taxpayer contended that United States securities owned by it could not lawfully be included in the tax base. With two justices dissenting, the Court upheld the tax, saying it was a tax in respect of the state-granted franchise, and it was immaterial that it was, in part, measured by ownership of federal obligations. The burden was too remote to be important. The same rationale sustained an inheritance tax measured in part by transmission of such obligations.[26] On the other hand, indirectness of the levy has been no excuse, if the real purpose was found to be to use the ownership of federal bonds to increase the tax. In *Missouri v. Gehner*,[27] the state laid a tax on insurance companies. The law provided that the base should be obtained by deducting from total assets the legal reserves and unpaid premium claims. However, the amount so deductible was to be reduced by a fraction, in which the amount

[23] Bank Tax Case; Bank v. Supervisors, *supra*, note 17; Home Savings Bank v. Des Moines, 205 U.S. 503 (1907); Farmers Bank v. Minnesota, 232 U.S. 516 (1914).

[24] The Banks v. The Mayor, *supra*, note 18.

[25] 134 U.S. 594 (1890).

[26] Plummer v. Coler, 178 U.S. 115 (1900).

[27] 281 U.S. 313 (1930).

of nontaxable United States bonds was the numerator and total assets the denominator. It was held the tax so ascertained was bad, as the law placed a heavier tax on companies owning such bonds than that imposed on others.[28] Three justices dissented.[29]

A levy on the interest received upon federal bonds is one step removed from a direct ad valorem tax on such bonds as assets of the taxpayer. Nevertheless, it has been held a direct burden, and so inadmissible. In *Northwestern Mutual Life Ins. Co.* v. *Wisconsin*,[30] the state imposed a license tax of 3 per cent of all interest received by insurance companies. The tax was declared by the statute to be in lieu of all taxes except those on real estate. In assessing the tax, the state included in the base interest received on United States bonds. To this extent the tax was held invalid. In its opinion, the Court said: "It has been settled doctrine here that, where principal is absolutely immune, no valid tax can be laid upon the income arising therefrom. To tax this would amount practically to laying a burden on the exempt principal." Soon after, however, the Court sustained a franchise tax on corporations measured by a percentage of net income, where interest from federal bonds was included in the base.[31] Here the burden was again thought too remote to matter.

Unquestionably, an employee of a department of the national government is a means, an agency, an instrumentality for executing that government's powers. Is an occupation tax assessed by the state of his residence a forbidden burden on the execution of its laws? At an early date the Court so held in *Dobbins* v. *Commissioners*.[32] The grounds of the decision

---

[28] Compare Macallen Co. v. Massachusetts, 279 U.S. 620 (1929); modified in Educational Films v. Ward, 282 U.S. 379 (1931).
[29] Hughes, C. J., concurred on the authority of National Life Ins. Co. v. United States, 277 U.S. 508 (1928).
[30] 275 U.S. 136 (1927).
[31] Educational Films v. Ward, 282 U.S. 379; three justices dissented.
[32] 16 Pet. 435 (1842).

were, first, that to allow such taxation would, in effect, be to give the states a revenue out of the revenue of the United States, "and to this they are not constitutionally entitled." This reasoning seems to leave something to be desired. Secondly, said the Court, the presumption is that the compensation is only such as will secure diligent performance of duty. Since it is the exclusive right of Congress to determine the amount of the employee's compensation, any state tax diminishing the amount of such compensation conflicts with the law of the United States which secures it to the employee in its entirety. Here there appears to be an ignoring of the dual citizenship of our people. Is every federal employee to be exempt from the burden of supporting, with all other citizens of a state, the services which the state supplies him?

This decision has not been overruled as to an occupation tax. But the reasoning by which the Court supported it has, after much wavering, been repudiated. *New York* v. *Graves*[33] declared the salary of an officer or employee of the Panama Railroad Company, a corporation wholly owned by the United States, exempt from a state tax on net income. But shortly thereafter in *Graves* v. *New York*,[34] it overruled the decision and held the salary of an employee of Home Owners' Loan Corporation, a federally owned corporation, not exempt from such a tax. This decision expressly overruled *New York* v. *Graves* and *Collector* v. *Day*.[35] It seems that *Dobbins* v. *Commissioners* ought to have gone with them, for I can see no difference between an occupation tax, a common though unscientific form of raising state revenue, and an income tax, so far as the burden on the federal government is concerned. Indeed, if the *Dobbins* case is good law, it is hard to see why the taxpayer was turned away in *Dyer* v. *Melrose*.[36] He was

[33] 299 U.S. 401 (1937).
[34] 306 U.S. 466 (1939).
[35] 11 Wall. 113 (1871). This case is discussed below.
[36] 215 U.S. 594 (1910).

a United States naval officer who deposited his pay in his bank and was assessed a state tax on it, along with all his other intangible property. His plea that he could still identify the sum as his government pay did not avail him to avoid its inclusion in his taxable assets.

Contracts and cash purchases by bureaus and departments are means of executing federal laws. Without them government would cease to function. Rather late it was asserted that to tax the transaction or the vendor for the transaction was to place an unconstitutional burden on the activities of the United States. The contention prevailed. In *Panhandle Oil Co.* v. *Knox*,[37] a state was precluded from collecting a sales tax on sales of gasoline to the United States for use by the Coast Guard; notwithstanding, the seller was the one required to report the sale and pay the tax. On the theory that the tax was passed on to the federal government, it was held to be an illegal burden. Four justices dissented. The decision was reaffirmed, over a dissent, in *Graves* v. *Texas Co.*[38] In the light of later cases these seem no longer to represent the law. See *Penn Dairies, Inc.* v. *Milk Control Comm.*, 318 U.S. 261, 269 (1943).

Meantime, it was attempted to have payments made under government contracts exempted on the ground that to tax the contractor upon the payment received was to tax the contract or the contractor, either being a federal instrumentality. In *Trinityfarm Construction Co.* v. *Grosjean*,[39] the Court rejected the contention that gasoline purchased by a contractor for use in building a levee under a contract with the United States should be exempt on the ground that he was a federal instrumentality. A much more debatable case, in the light of the earlier decisions, was *James* v. *Dravo Contracting Co.*,[40] where one performing a contract for the United States

---

[37] 277 U.S. 218 (1928).
[38] 298 U.S. 393 (1936).
[39] 291 U.S. 466 (1934).
[40] 302 U.S. 134 (1937).

claimed exemption of the consideration paid him from a state gross-receipts tax. It was claimed that the tax was invalid as laid on the contract itself or on the contractor as a federal instrumentality. But the Court sustained the tax on the ground that the burden on the government was incidental, indirect, remote, and inconsequential. The opinion of the Court labored valiantly, and, as I think, unsuccessfully, to distinguish the earlier cases. On the same day the Court upheld a state occupation tax imposed on another government contractor measured by gross receipts including the gross receipts of the government contract.[41] These decisions were followed in *Atkinson* v. *State Tax Commission*,[42] sustaining a state income tax which included in its base profits from work on a federal project. Later decisions were but a gloss on what had been ruled in those mentioned. In *Alabama* v. *King and Boozer*,[43] the state sought to impose a sales tax on the purchase of materials by contractors who were supplying the government on a cost-plus contract, which provided that the United States would reimburse the contractor for taxes paid. It was held that the imposition of the tax laid no unconstitutional burden on the federal government, though it was admitted that the "economic burden" of the exaction fell upon it.[44]

After all this comes the capstone of confusion. During World War II the United States, in order to speed production of essential war materials, made contracts with producers under the terms of which machinery was to be bailed to the contractor by the government. By the terms of these contracts such machinery was to remain the property of the government and was to be kept clear of liens and incumbrances. Under one of these contracts machinery was supplied to a

[41] Silas Mason Co. v. State Tax Commission, 302 U.S. 186 (1937).
[42] 303 U.S. 20 (1938).
[43] 314 U.S. 1 (1941).
[44] A like holding sustained a use tax on materials purchased by the contractor under a like contract: Curry v. United States, 314 U.S. 14 (1941).

contractor in Pennsylvania. At the ensuing assessment of real estate for local taxation, the assessors raised the assessment of the contractor's real estate (land, buildings, and fixtures), in some measure owing to the installation of machinery supplied him by the government under the contract. He resisted the assessment on the ground that to increase it by reason of the installation of property of the United States was to tax an instrumentality of the United States. In view of uniform state decisions that, while the state could not tax the bailor's machinery or subject it to execution or sale for default in payment, it could increase the real estate tax of the bailee by reason of his installation and use of the machinery, the state court sustained the increased assessment. The Supreme Court reversed the decision in *United States* v. *County of Allegheny*.[45]

It is difficult to justify the result in the light of the progressive subjection of contractors to nondiscriminatory state taxation on the proceeds of contracts with the United States, or on their property used in performance of the contract. The tax was not a direct tax on the property of the United States, as the Court held. It seems that, in effect, the Court has reintroduced, under the formula of direct taxation, the discarded test of economic burden.

An interesting phase of the doctrine of immunity springs from the decision in *McCulloch* v. *Maryland*.[46] For no reason that I can imagine, except a concept of statesmanship in the treatment of the relation of nation and state, the Court there announced that state taxation of the property of a federal instrumentality is permissible. The Chief Justice said that the Court's opinion "does not extend to a tax paid by the real property of the bank, in common with other real property within the state." But such taxation surely is a burden.

Nothing in the opinion limits the permitted exercise of

[45] 322 U.S. 174 (1944).   [46] *Supra*, note 4.

power to mere agencies of the United States. It is not seen how there can be any difference, in principle or in result, between taxing for local purposes the property of the United States and that of one of its instrumentalities. Yet the distinction has been observed until recently. After *McCulloch* v. *Maryland*, the Court, several times, upheld state taxation of the property of a federal agency or instrumentality. In *Thomson* v. *Union Pacific R.R.*,[47] a railroad company organized by a territory which the Court held served a national purpose under contracts with the United States was held liable to local taxes on its property, and in *Union Pacific R.R.* v. *Peniston*,[48] a railroad company chartered by Congress and operating under contract as an agent of the federal government was held amenable to like state taxation. Later, the Court held that the equipment used by a contractor with the United States might be subjected to local taxation.[49]

In *Alward* v. *Johnson*,[50] the taxpayer had a contract to carry the United States mails. He used his own automobile. California laid a tax on all carriers of passengers and freight of a percentage of the carrier's gross receipts. The statute imposing it recited that the tax was in lieu of all other taxes on the taxpayer's property. It was claimed the tax was void as to the mail carrier because he was a federal instrumentality. The state court sustained the levy as a tax on property. The Supreme Court affirmed, saying: "There was no tax upon the contract for such carriage; the burden laid upon the property employed affected operations of the federal government only remotely."

The doctrine was modified in *Clallam County* v. *United States*.[51] There it appeared that in order to promote the war

[47] 9 Wall. 579 (1869).
[48] 18 Wall. 5 (1873).
[49] Gromer v. Standard Dredging Co., 224 U.S. 362 (1912).
[50] 282 U.S. 509 (1931).
[51] 263 U.S. 341 (1923).

effort in World War I, the United States caused a corporation to be organized under the laws of the State of Washington to manufacture airplane parts from spruce lumber. Under the plan the entire capital stock and all the bonds issued by the company were owned by the United States. The corporation was to be wound up at the conclusion of the war. The county demanded a tax on the company's real estate at the uniform rate exacted from owners of real property. The Supreme Court held the company was exempt from this tax. Mr. Justice Holmes wrote the opinion, which, I submit, was wholly vague as to the reasons for the decision. After reciting the facts, he said:

"This is not like the case of a corporation having its own purposes as well as those of the United States and interested in profit on its own account. The incorporation and formal erection of a new personality was only for the convenience of the United States to carry out its ends. It is unnecessary to consider whether the fact that the United States owned all the stock and furnished all the property to the corporation taken by itself would be enough to bring the case within the policy of the rule that exempts property of the United States. *Van Brocklin* v. *Tennessee* (*Van Brocklin* v. *Anderson*), 117 U.S. 151. It may be that if the United States saw fit to avail itself of machinery furnished by the state it would not escape the tax on that ground alone. But when we add the facts that we have recited we think it too plain for further argument that the tax could not be imposed."

Whether an exception is to be made to the rule announced in *McCulloch* v. *Maryland* when the nation is in war, or where the whole capital of the agency is owned by the United States, we are not told.

It remains to discuss the two most puzzling chapters in the course of the Court's efforts to mark the line of prohibited taxation. The first is its dealing with the fruits of patents and copyrights; the second, its views regarding lessees of lands held by the United States as guardian of the Indians.

In 1927 a state asserted a claim for an income tax in respect of royalties received from licenses of a United States patent. The taxpayer claimed exemption on the ground that a patent is a federal instrumentality, and his claim was sustained by a sharply divided Court.[52] It is to be observed that the ruling was in accord with Chief Justice Marshall's statement in the *McCulloch* case that a contrary ruling would permit states to "tax patent rights" and the uniform holdings that a tax on the income of property is a tax on the property itself.

Four years later another taxpayer, taking a leaf out of the former's book, asserted a claim to immunity from a gross-receipts tax which was asserted against royalties of copyrights.[53] This time a unanimous Court rejected his contention and overruled the earlier decision.

In 1914 a lessee under a mineral lease of Indian lands, leased to him on royalty by the United States as guardian, successfully asserted an immunity from a state occupation or privilege tax of a percentage of gross income from the minerals extracted.[54]

There ensued a series of cases applying the ruling to varying forms of state taxation incident to such leases.[55] This taxation ran the gamut from a tax on the lease or on the oil produced to one on the net income of the lessee. All these cases have been overruled.[56]

---

[52] Long v. Rockwood, 277 U.S. 142 (1928).

[53] Fox Film Corp. v. Doyal, 286 U.S. 123 (1932).

[54] Choctaw, Oklahoma & Gulf R.R. v. Harrison, 235 U.S. 292 (1914).

[55] Indian Terr. Ill. Oil Co. v. Oklahoma, 240 U.S. 522 (1916); Howard v. Gipsy Oil Co., 247 U.S. 503 (1918); Large Oil Co. v. Howard, 248 U.S. 549 (1919); Gillespie v. Oklahoma, 257 U.S. 501 (1922).

[56] Helvering v. Mountain Producers Corp., 303 U.S. 376, 387 (1938); Oklahoma Tax Comm. v. Texas Co., 336 U.S. 342, 365 (1949).

We turn now to the other side of the shield and inquire whether the immunity of a state from federal taxation is as broad as the federal immunity we have discussed. In the light of the repeated statements that state and nation are each sovereign in its own field, we might expect that there would be a close correspondence between the reciprocal immunities. Comparison can best be made by considering separately the same classes of means or agencies as were considered under the topic of federal immunity. It appears always to have been conceded that a tax laid directly on bonds of a state is invalid. The principle has been extended to a federal income tax applied to interest on municipal bonds.[57] The same principle was applied to a federal tax on interest received by life insurance companies where the levy included interest on state bonds.[58] The Court said: "Directly to tax the income from securities amounts to taxation of the securities themselves."

On the other hand, as in the case of state taxation, the federal excise tax on corporations is not invalidated by the fact that the taxed corporation owns state or municipal bonds.[59] Likewise, following the same rule announced in the case of state taxation, it has been held that federal transfer, inheritance, and gift taxes may be imposed, although part of the principal involved consists of state securities.[60] The same rule has been announced in the case of a capital gains tax.[61]

It has been held that interest due a state or one of its municipalities is beyond the reach of the federal taxing power. In *United States v. Baltimore & Ohio R.R.*,[62] a city, in order to aid and encourage the building of the railroad, exercised a

[57] Pollock v. Farmers' Loan & Trust Co., 157 U.S. 429 (1895).
[58] National Life Insurance Co. v. United States, 277 U.S. 508 (1928).
[59] Flint v. Stone Tracy Co., 220 U.S. 107 (1911).
[60] Knowlton v. Moore, 178 U.S. 41 (1900); Snyder v. Bettman, 190 U.S. 249 (1903); N.Y. Trust Co. v. Eisner, 256 U.S. 345 (1921); Greiner v. Lewellyn, 258 U.S. 384 (1922).
[61] Willcuts v. Bunn, 282 U.S. 216 (1931).
[62] 17 Wall. 322 (1872).

power conferred on it by the state and sold $5,000,000 of bonds, the proceeds of which it turned over to the railroad. To indemnify the city, the railroad executed a mortgage to the city for the amount advanced and interest. The federal tax law provided that the debtor should deduct the tax from any interest paid. The question was whether the railroad must deduct and pay to the United States the tax on the interest paid to the city. It was held that the tax was not on the railroad but on the owner of the bonds and that "the city was an arm of the state and entitled to the same exemption as the state," and refund of the tax paid was ordered.

We come next to the question of taxes laid upon officials of state governments or their compensation. Some years after the Court had held that a federal officer could not be made liable for an occupation tax levied by the community in which he lived,[63] the Court made a similar ruling with respect to a federal tax on the salary of a state judge in *Collector* v. *Day*.[64] Mr. Justice Bradley dissented, pointing out that although the judge was an official of the state performing functions necessary to the operation of state government, he, nevertheless, was a citizen of the United States and bound to contribute, with all other citizens, no matter in what state domiciled, his proper share for the support of that government. Under the force of the decision in *Collector* v. *Day*, state officials were exempt from federal taxation either on their occupations or on so much of their income as came to them in the form of official salaries until the case was overruled after seventy years in *Graves* v. *New York*.[65] In *Flint* v. *Stone Tracy Co.*,[66] it had been held that corporations acting as trustees or guardians under authority of the laws or the courts of a state were not agents of the state in such sense that they were

[63] Dobbins v. Commissioners, *supra*, note 32.
[64] 11 Wall. 113 (1871).
[65] 306 U.S. 466 (1939).
[66] *Supra*, note 7.

exempt from the federal excise tax on corporations. In *Metcalf and Eddy* v. *Mitchell*,[67] engineers who rendered consulting services under a contract with the state were held liable for federal income tax where the base included the sums received for their services. The basis of decision was that it was not made to appear that the tax substantially impaired the ability of the retained engineer to discharge his obligations or the ability of the state to procure such services to aid in the performance of state undertakings. This was the reverse of the ruling in the *Dobbins* case. On the other hand, the salary of the chief engineer of the New York Bureau of Water Supply was held immune from federal income tax, though over a dissent.[68]

And, as in the case of trust companies acting as fiduciaries, so the compensation of attorneys for winding up a corporation under state law and under the direction of state officials was held subject to federal income tax.[69] The basis of decision was the remoteness of the burden on the state.

Immediately afterward, the Court held that employees of the New York Port Authority, a joint public-service undertaking of the states of New Jersey and New York, were liable for federal income tax in respect of their salaries. This decision overruled *Collector* v. *Day* and carried with it *Brush* v. *Commissioner*.[70]

It has been noted that state sales taxes on materials purchased by government bureaus and departments were for a period held invalid as a burden on the operation of the federal government. During the period when these decisions were in force, a similar holding was made in the reverse situation where a federal excise tax was sought to be imposed on sales to a municipality of motorcycles to be used by the

[67] 269 U.S. 514 (1926).
[68] Brush v. Commissioner, 300 U.S. 352 (1937).
[69] Helvering v. Therrell, 303 U.S. 218 (1938).
[70] Graves v. New York, *supra*, note 34.

police force.[71] While this decision has never been specifically overruled, it would seem no longer binding in view of the virtual reversal of the cases involving state sales taxes on sales to the federal government.

The analogue of the lease cases which prohibited taxation of the activities of lessees of the federal government is found in *Burnet* v. *Coronado Oil and Gas Co.*,[72] in which it appeared that school lands owned by a state had been leased for the extraction of minerals. A federal net income tax was demanded of the lessee. He objected to paying so much of the tax as represented income from operation of the lease. His objection was sustained. It was held that the lease was an instrumentality of the state in the exercise of a governmental function and could not, therefore, be burdened by the federal tax. In this field, too, the Court pursued a wavering policy. In one case,[73] it sustained income taxation against a lessee of state lands, because under the state law a lease of oil and gas was construed a sale of minerals in place. It was, therefore, held that the lessee was selling his own property and that no question of instrumentality was involved. In another case, the Court endeavored to distinguish *Gillespie* v. *Oklahoma*[74] in a case which was really indistinguishable.[75]

As in the reverse situation of state taxation in respect of federal leases, the Court finally came to a definite position. In *Helvering* v. *Mountain Producers Corp.*,[76] a producer of oil and gas under a lease of state lands was held to have no immunity from federal income tax. The decision was grounded on the remoteness of any burden or interference with the functions of the state government.

[71] Indian Motorcycle Co. v. United States, 283 U.S. 570 (1931).
[72] 285 U.S. 393 (1932).
[73] Group No. 1 Oil Corp. v. Bass, 283 U.S. 279 (1931).
[74] *Supra*, note 55.
[75] Burnet v. Jergins Trust, 288 U.S. 508 (1933).
[76] 303 U.S. 376 (1938).

The last series of cases to be considered presents perhaps the most difficult situation that has faced the Court. These have arisen where a state or one of its municipalities has determined on grounds of public policy that the public should take over a business as the best means of regulating it. Many states have determined that as a matter of government policy the liquor business should be handled by the state, so that citizens cannot buy liquor except through a controlled state agency. The question arises may the federal government impose an excise tax on such state activity. In *South Carolina* v. *United States*,[77] the Court answered in the affirmative. It put its decision on the ground that the activity in question was not strictly governmental and limited exemption to activities so characterized. The decision was followed some years later in *Ohio* v. *Helvering*,[78] where, again, it was held that when a state engages in a business of a private nature it exercises a nongovernmental function and its activity, therefore, is not immune from federal taxation. In *Helvering* v. *Powers*,[79] the Court reached the conclusion that one employed as a manager or superintendent of a state-operated street-railway system could not claim exemption from income tax on the salary paid him in that capacity. The Court, however, put the case, not on the remoteness of burden, but on the ground that the activity of the state was not governmental, but was of the nature of a private business, and therefore any of its activities were subject to federal taxation. Again in *Allen* v. *Regents*,[80] the Court held that the regents of a state university were liable for a federal admissions tax on tickets sold for intercollegiate contests. The regents showed that the university was a state institution and that the expense of its physical education and athletic programs was largely defrayed from the admissions charged to the

---

[77] 199 U.S. 437 (1905).
[78] 292 U.S. 360 (1934).
[79] 293 U.S. 214 (1934).
[80] 304 U.S. 439 (1938).

contests. It was not easy for the Court to follow the line that the activity in question was a nongovernmental one. It can hardly be said that there was an opinion by the Court. One justice did not participate, three concurred in the result, and two dissented.

The last and by odds the most difficult problem in this field was presented in *New York* v. *United States*.[81] In this case, the State of New York owned a tract, devoted to recreation, which contained mineral springs. The state bottled and sold the mineral waters from these springs. The United States had enacted a law levying an excise on the sale of bottled mineral water. The state resisted payment of a tax imposed under that law.

The tax was sustained. That, however, is about all that can be said of the case. Mr. Justice Frankfurter proposed this formula: that where the government seeks to place an excise on a business commonly conducted by private interests, it may say to a state, if you engage in that sort of business in competition with other citizens you must pay the same tax they pay. He laid it down as a test of validity that the tax must not discriminate, that is, be aimed exclusively at a state activity. Mr. Justice Rutledge concurred in this opinion but added some further considerations. Four other justices joined in sustaining the tax under the facts disclosed in the case, but they were not satisfied that mere lack of discrimination was sufficient to validate a federal tax laid on a state activity or state property. Their view was that some forms of tax, however evenly distributed over the persons or the property involved, may nevertheless be unenforceable against a state instrumentality or state property. Mr. Justice Douglas and Mr. Justice Black dissented, holding that *South Carolina* v. *United States* should be overruled. They contended that even the sale of bottled waters as conducted by New York was a govern-

[81] 326 U.S. 572 (1946).

mental function and therefore immune from taxation by the federal government. Mr. Justice Jackson took no part in the decision.

The varying opinions leave us with no certainty except that a discriminatory tax aimed by the federal government at a state activity to the exclusion of similar activities conducted by others would be bad. This seems obvious. As to nondiscriminatory federal taxes involving state activities, we are left with little to guide us.

After this somewhat discursive account of the course of decision, perhaps we may draw some conclusions and venture some comments.

First: It seems settled that neither sovereign may tax the other's property. Is the rule necessary to our federal system, and is it just? Each of us acknowledges the same two sovereigns, the state government and the federal government. If the latter acquires real estate within a given state, the property involved receives services from the state or its agencies which are essential and valuable, which cost the taxpayers of the state or municipality substantial sums for their rendition. A customhouse or a post-office building, for instance, demands and receives from the community in which it is located the establishment and maintenance of streets and roads, water supply and sewage disposal, police and fire protection, and other public services. These are necessarily rendered at the expense of the local taxpaying community. It seems an unfair discrimination that the citizens of one state or one city, who constitute but a small segment of the citizens of the United States, should be called upon to render at their own expense special services to the whole body of United States citizens.

In a very real sense, therefore, the arbitrary rule which exempts the United States from state taxation of its property works a special discrimination between citizens of different states and between groups of citizens of the United States.

Moreover, the great expansion of federal activities—Boulder Dams and Tennessee Valley Authorities, for example—may result in withdrawing from a state's tax roll so much property as to seriously embarrass its government. And if the *Clallam County* decision[82] extends the immunity to the property of all corporations whose stock is wholly owned by the United States, the plight of the states is worse.

Secondly: There has been no variation of the rule that federal and state securities and the interest on them are exempt. Is this rule necessary to the preservation of nation and state, and is it just?

In the light of the course of decision on other claims of immunity, I believe that this one needs reëxamination. In every instance where taxation of a federal or state agency has been held invalid, it is possible to spell out some burden. Where such a burden has been held permissible, this has been by characterizing it as indirect, remote, or incidental. I admit that a tax on United States bonds as property is direct rather than remote, but, assuming that this is so, is it any less direct or remote than an occupation tax assessed by a state on the occupation of a postmaster? Is it more or less burdensome than such an occupation tax, or an income tax in which the official's salary is included? How can one say? The argument is that a government can borrow on better terms if the securities it issues and the interest on those securities are exempt from tax. This is probably true. Several considerations, however, ought to be held in mind. The federal government does not hesitate to tax the income from its own securities. This must be upon the theory that citizens of the United States ought to pay taxes on all income from investments of whatever nature. The states are free to tax their own bonds as property or to tax the income therefrom. Such taxation would

[82] *Supra*, note 51.

again be upon the theory that all the assets or income of a citizen should bear an appropriate share of the cost of government. Now that federal income taxation has reached very high levels in the upper income brackets, the effect of the exemption is unhealthy. It is driving many investors into the public bond field to the exclusion of other investment. This may have a serious effect on our economy. The exemption of large incomes, or very large segments of individual income, from taxation is working a real discrimination against those who would invest their capital in productive private enterprise.

The reasoning of Mr. Justice Bradley in his dissenting opinion in *Collector* v. *Day*[83] seems to be the answer to this problem. As he said, an individual is equally a citizen of the United States and of his own state. He ought fairly to share the cost of the government of both. And, as Mr. Justice Thompson said in *Weston* v. *Charleston*,[84] if a citizen is liable to taxation on his money, as such, it is not logical that one who invests that money in an interest-bearing security of the federal government should become exempt to that extent from his fair share of the burden of local government. The principle is equally applicable to investment in state securities. It is a serious question whether this immunity should not be abolished.

Thirdly: It seemed, until the decision in the *Allegheny County* case,[85] that "economic burden" had been banned as a test of invalidity of a tax on a government agency. Certainly it should be. But there remain instances like the *Dobbins* case where "directness" still turns the scale against the tax. Why are not all state employees obliged to pay their fair share of federal costs and all federal employees obliged to pay their fair share of local costs? It would have been well

[83] *Supra*, note 64.
[84] 2 Pet. at p. 477 (1829).
[85] *Supra*, note 45.

if Mr. Justice Bradley's views expressed in *Collector* v. *Day* [86] had been those of the Court.

Fourthly: It is right that vendors to or contractors with state and federal governments should not be exempt from excise or income taxes based on their sales to or receipts from government. And so of lessees of land from either sovereign. Owners of patents and copyrights should not be exempt from state taxes on royalty income from them. It will hardly be suggested that an ad valorem tax on them would be bad because more "direct."

"Direct" and "indirect," "remote" and "incidental," "governmental" and "proprietary" have all been used to justify decisions one way or the other. Once in a while we are adjured to be "practical" in dealing with alleged obstruction of governmental functions. And often the touchstone is said to be "discrimination." However, in *New York* v. *United States*,[87] four justices, while admitting that a law of one sovereign that selected an activity of the other and taxed that alone would be bad for discrimination, insisted that a nondiscriminatory tax might also be bad if applied to objects which ought to be exempt. Yet it still is the law that the federal government may by discriminatory taxes suppress a practice or an article whether deemed to interfere with a federal power[88] or having no relation to such power, so that it could not otherwise be regulated.[89]

Most of the immunities so carefully built up on *McCulloch* v. *Maryland* have subsequently been swept away. In any practical view of the subject, more should go.

But there remain, as will probably always be so, areas of doubt and dispute. One of these is created by the growing expansion of national and state activities. Perhaps it is still

[86] 11 Wall. at p. 128.
[87] *Supra*, note 81.
[88] Veazie Bank v. Fenno, *supra*, note 5.
[89] McCray v. United States, *supra*, note 6.

true that if a state takes over the liquor business, or the transportation business, or sells tickets for a state institution's benefit, or sells mineral water emanating from its own lands, it must pay taxes which federal law has laid on the conduct of such activities without exempting state agencies. That the state is liable for such taxes and the reasons for such liability are still matters of active and pointed debate.

One other matter calls for notice. A question that has obtruded itself but never been decided is whether Congress can, by legislative fiat, immunize any of the activities of persons the Court has held amenable to state taxation. In several instances, Congress has essayed to immunize property or transactions of agencies created by it. Some of these statutory immunities have been challenged by suits. But in these cases it was clear that the immunity declared by Congress was justified on the principles theretofore judicially announced,[90] though some of the language used was broader than the facts demanded. What if Congress attempts to immunize government contracts or contractors from state sales taxes or gross or net income taxes in respect of transactions with the United States? Must the Court enforce the Congressional will? This has never been decided. The opinions merely note that the question may arise.[91]

Mr. Justice Frankfurter, however, in the *Allegheny County* case, while holding that, on the facts presented, the taxpayer was not immune from the state tax, said: "I have no doubt that Congress, by appropriate legislation could immunize those who deal with the Government from sales and property taxes which States otherwise are free to impose."

[90] *E.g.*, Smith v. Kansas City Title & Trust Co., 255 U.S. 180 (1921); Federal Land Bank v. Crosland, 261 U.S. 374 (1922); Pittman v. Home Owners' Loan Corp., 308 U.S. 21 (1939); Federal Land Bank v. Bismarck Lumber Co., 314 U.S. 95 (1941).
[91] Shaw v. Oil Corp., 276 U.S. 575, 579, 581 (1928); Alabama v. King & Boozer, 314 U.S. 1, 8 (1941); Oklahoma Tax. Comm. v. Texas Co., 336 U.S. 342, 365 (1949).

I cannot agree. The power to decide is in the Court and nowhere else. It would be to make a mockery of state sovereignty if Congress could override it at will beyond redress in the Court in which is reposed the decision of cases arising under the Constitution. So to hold would, in effect, be to make Congress the final arbiter, to the destruction of the national harmony, the preservation of which the Constitution commits to the judiciary.

New and difficult problems seek an answer. They arise from the expanded activities of state and national governments which were not envisaged when the Constitution was adopted or when the early decisions of the Court in the field of intergovernmental taxation were announced. As I have noted, the federal government, in the exercise of its granted powers, has established public works of enormous magnitude and will probably continue to do so. From many of these the government receives very substantial revenue, derived from activities within the confines of a state. On the other hand, in order to supply the service the public is deemed to need, the states are going into great enterprises of conservation, transportation, including toll roads and toll bridges, and the conduct of many activities heretofore classed as businesses. In many of these cases the moneys borrowed for the enterprize are to be repaid by tolls and fees collected from users, and the users are by no means confined to citizens of the states in question. Are all these instrumentalities of state and nation to be, as the opinion in *McCulloch* v. *Maryland* would indicate, completely free of taxation by the other sovereign? Are they to bear like taxation as citizens do who conduct like enterprizes; is there to be a distinction between the property employed, if taxed on an equal basis with all other property, and activities pursued; is a tax on the activity of one of these agencies so like a franchise tax in corporate activity that there is no propriety in any immunity? How far in any of these cases should the result be governed by an attempt to calculate the financial result to the respective government—beneficial or detrimental—of abolishing immunity?

These and similar questions are still to be mooted. My own view is that the steady progress toward the abolition of the reciprocal immunities has been beneficial. Much of what was involved in the opinion in *McCulloch* v. *Maryland*, for a time adopted by the Court, has been thrown overboard. It is pertinent to ask whether Chief Justice Marshall was not wrong when he said that the question was not one of "confidence" but one of power. Save for obvious discrimination, why is not the citizen of dual sovereigns entitled to repose confidence that neither of those sovereigns can or will, by nondiscriminatory taxation of its own citizens, destroy or hamper the operations of the other?

II. Conflicts of Police Power

When the Constitution was adopted the states possessed what lawyers style the "police power." It means the power to regulate the conduct and relations of the members of society. In effect, it means the general power of legislation. At first blush, it would seem that the federal government has no such power, but upon examining the grants to Congress we find that one of them is of the power "to regulate commerce . . . among the several states."

This power vested in Congress is superior, within the designated field, to any regulatory power of the states. The Supreme Court has declared "the authority of the federal government over interstate commerce does not differ in extent or character from that retained by the states over intrastate commerce."[1] In short, both a state and the nation may exercise the police power, the former without restriction, save as the authority granted to the federal government limits its action.

The term "commerce," used in Article I, Section 8, of the Constitution, has been declared by the Court to be equivalent to the phrase "intercourse for the purpose of trade," and includes transportation, purchase, sale, and exchange of commodities between the citizens of the different states.[2] "Regula-

[1] United States v. Rock Royal Co-operative, 307 U.S. 533, 569 (1939).
[2] Carter v. Carter Coal Co., 298 U.S. 238, 298 (1936).

tion" has been defined as the declaring of the rule by which commerce is to be governed,[3] and embraces measures intended to foster and protect commerce between the states,[4] including those which prohibit commerce in certain commodities.[5]

The exercise of the power of Congress to regulate can neither be enlarged nor circumscribed by state action.[6] Congress has the choice whether to prescribe that which supports state policy or that which runs counter to it.

What is the permissible exercise of the state's police power in the light of the commerce clause of the Constitution, and what is the role of the Supreme Court in preventing state action from trespassing on the field of federal competence or federal action from invading the general police power of a state?

Three situations have arisen calling for decision by the Court as to the limits of state power. They are presented, first, where Congress has by valid legislation taken over the regulation of a given area. Here, the action of Congress within the orbit of the commerce power supersedes existing state law and precludes future regulation of the subject by state authority,[7] but does not prevent state regulation of local matters which, though they touch interstate commerce, do not interfere with the operation of federal regulation[8] or, while in the same field, deal with matters of local competence not touched by the federal action.[9]

Secondly, in a wide range of local regulation, as, for ex-

[3] Gibbons v. Ogden, 9 Wheat. 1, 196 (1824).
[4] The Daniel Ball, 10 Wall. 557, 564 (1871); Mobile County v. Kimball, 102 U.S. 691 (1880); Second Employers' Liability Cases, 223 U.S. 1 (1912).
[5] United States v. Carolene Products Co., 304 U.S. 144 (1938).
[6] United States v. Darby, 312 U.S. 100, 114 (1941).
[7] Cloverleaf Butter Co. v. Patterson, 315 U.S. 148 (1942).
[8] South Carolina State Highway Dept. v. Barnwell Bros., 303 U.S. 177 (1938); Terminal R.R. Assn. v. Brotherhood, 318 U.S. 1 (1943).
[9] Arkansas Louisiana Gas Co. v. Dept. of Public Utilities, 304 U.S. 61 (1938); California v. Thompson, 313 U.S. 109 (1941).

ample, matters of health and safety, the states are free to act until Congress enters the field by prescribing a uniform national rule.[10]

Thirdly, there are cases where the subject of state regulation is unquestionably within the scope of interstate commerce, where although Congress has failed to express any policy the claim is that the state's action infringes the federal jurisdiction.

In all these cases the Court is called on to adjudicate the respective claims of state and nation. In the first, the question is, has Congress by its legislation so occupied the field as to exclude state regulation? This is merely a matter of statutory construction. In the second, the issue is whether the action of Congress precludes state legislation consistent with the federal regulation. This matter raises no constitutional question. In the third, the Court has no aid as to Congressional policy. Here it has to define the area of state power only as a corollary of the supremacy of the commerce power. The Congress has, for whatever reason, not exercised its power of regulation. In such cases, the Court has essayed to determine whether the state regulation interferes with interstate commerce.

Thus, though Congress has not legislated on the subject, it has been held that a state may not tax the transaction of interstate business[11] and may not impose burdensome regulations on that business.[12] Nor can the state interfere with or obstruct interstate travel.[13]

[10] Maurer v. Hamilton, 309 U.S. 598 (1940); Ziffrin v. Reeves, 308 U.S. 132 (1939).

[11] Illinois Cent. R.R. v. Minnesota, 309 U.S. 157 (1940); McCarroll v. Dixie Greyhound Lines, 309 U.S. 176 (1940); McGoldrick v. Gulf Oil Corp., 309 U.S. 414 (1940); New Jersey Bell Tel. Co. v. State Board, 280 U.S. 338 (1930).

[12] Lemke v. Farmers' Grain Co., 258 U.S. 50 (1922); Southern Pacific Co. v. Arizona, 325 U.S. 761 (1945); Nippert v. Richmond, 327 U.S. 416 (1946); Joseph v. Carter & Weekes Co., 330 U.S. 422 (1947).

[13] Edwards v. California, 314 U.S. 160 (1941).

The Court has, on the other hand, considered that its function included the determination whether Congress has exceeded its granted power in attempting to regulate local transactions under the guise of the regulation of interstate commerce.[14] Often it has avoided a decision to this effect by holding that the statute does not cover the transaction in question.[15]

At first, Congressional regulation was largely confined to prohibition of interstate shipment of some commodity deemed injurious to public morals[16] or to public health[17] or to economic welfare,[18] and Congressional enactments, barring interstate transportation of white slaves, stolen automoblies, or kidnapped persons, have been sustained as valid regulations. A convenient catalogue of such statutes and the decisions upholding them will be found in the opinion in *Kentucky Whip and Collar Co.* v. *Illinois Central R.R.*[19]

As our economy developed, regulation took a broader sweep. Congress adopted the Sherman Antitrust Act to deal with conspiracies in restraint of interstate trade and monopolies of such trade. This was an extension over earlier legislation concerning interstate commerce, for such activities might be local and still adversely affect interstate competition. To the contention that because they were local and so beyond the competence of Congress under the commerce clause, the Court turned a deaf ear.[20]

The Sherman Act declared the legislative policy in broad

[14] *E.g.*, United States v. De Witt, 9 Wall. 41 (1870); Keller v. United States, 213 U.S. 138 (1909); Child Labor Tax Case, 259 U.S. 20 (1922); A. L. A. Schecter Corp. v. United States, 295 U.S. 495 (1935).

[15] Higgins v. Carr Brothers Co., 317 U.S. 572 (1943).

[16] Lottery Case, 188 U.S. 321 (1903).

[17] Reid v. Colorado, 187 U.S. 137 (1902).

[18] United States v. Delaware & Hudson Co., 213 U.S. 366 (1909).

[19] 299 U.S. 334, at p. 346 (1937).

[20] Standard Oil Co. v. United States, 221 U.S. 1 (1911); United Mine Workers v. Coronado Coal Co., 259 U.S. 344 (1922).

terms and left enforcement to the courts in civil suits or criminal prosecutions initiated by the government, or in a civil action by one damaged by violation of the statute.

In 1890 Congress, having determined it would be impractical to regulate by statute all of the details of the business of interstate carriage by rail, and all the rates and practices of interstate railroads, adopted a new technique. In the Interstate Commerce Act it laid down broad principles touching the subject and created an administrative body to which it delegated the function of investigation and of hearing complaints, of promulgating rules and issuing orders banning practices inconsistent with the mandate of the statute, subject to court review. The validity of this method of regulation in broad fields of activity, by delegation, is beyond question. The judicial controversies which result are largely on the issue whether the administrative body has kept within the principles and rules laid down in the statute.

Thus by the end of the last century there had come to be three recognized types of regulation. First, the interdiction by criminal statute of interstate transportation of specified commodities or persons. Secondly, the interdiction of concerted action, wherever localized, directed at the destruction of free competition in interstate trade. And, thirdly, regulation of activities of those engaged in interstate transportation by the aid of a legislative delegate, which should implement and enforce the declared purpose of Congress.

From the first, it has been understood that state action, though authorized or required by state law, if in conflict with a valid exercise of the commerce power by Congress, must give way; and this is so although, except for the exercise of the power of Congress, the state regulation would be valid. Thus, in order to effectuate the commerce power of the federal government, it may become necessary to modify or abrogate state action.

A classical illustration of this principle was furnished by the *Shreveport Case*.[21] There the Interstate Commerce Commission prescribed rates which it found to be just and reasonable for interstate carriage by interstate railroads whose lines traversed the State of Texas. Under state law these carriers maintained much lower rates for comparable service intrastate, so that there resulted substantial discrimination between the interstate and the intrastate rates applicable to certain points within Texas. The Commission, exercising authority conferred on it, found that in order to remove this discrimination the intrastate rates must be raised to the level of the interstate rates it had prescribed; and it entered an order requiring the carriers to equalize the intrastate rates with the interstate. The railroads sued in a federal court to set aside the Commission's order on the ground that it exceeded Congress' constitutional authority. They contended that Congress was impotent to control intrastate charges of an interstate carrier, even though it found such control necessary to prevent injurious discrimination against interstate traffic.

The Court, in overruling the contention, said: "The fact that carriers are instruments of intrastate commerce as well as of interstate commerce does not derogate from the complete and paramount authority of Congress over the latter, or preclude the federal power from being exerted to prevent the intrastate operations of such carriers from being made a means of injury to that which has been confided to the federal government."

In support of its position, the Court adverted to the fact that it had sustained the Hours of Service Act, by which Congress fixed the hours of service of employees in interstate transportation, although employees dealing with the movement of trains who were made subject to the act were employed in both interstate and intrastate commerce. This was

[21] 234 U.S. 342 (1914).

on the ground that the will of Congress as to hours of service in interstate transportation could not be defeated by the commingling of duties relating to both interstate and intrastate operations.[22] The Court also relied on the decision that a Safety Appliance Act, though not confined to vehicles used solely in interstate traffic, was a valid regulation because the close relationship between the two classes of traffic moving over the same line of railroad required the provisions of the act to extend to both classes of vehicles.[23]

There can be no question of the correctness of the decision in the *Shreveport Case*. The power to regulate the interstate rates was incontestable. But if action required by state law, in carriage within the state, were to be allowed to disrupt and destroy the efficacy of the order regarding interstate rates, the power of the national legislature under the commerce clause would be nullified.

The question arose whether Congress could go beyond the point reached in the *Shreveport Case*. In a series of cases the Court had declared that manufacturing, mining, or any form of production, were purely local activities not subject to regulation under the commerce power.[24] In the light of the earlier of these decisions, the Congress had essayed in vain to regulate a local activity solely on the ground that, if unregulated, it would interfere with interstate commerce.[25] It had attempted, in vain, to regulate local activities in the interest of interstate commerce by penalizing with heavy tax-

[22] Baltimore & Ohio R.R. v. Interstate Commerce Commission, 221 U.S. 612 (1911).

[23] Southern Ry. v. United States, 222 U.S. 20 (1911).

[24] United States v. E. C. Knight Co., 156 U.S. 1, 12, 13 (1895); Kidd v. Pearson, 128 U.S. 1, 20, 21, 22 (1888); Hopkins v. United States, 171 U.S. 578 (1898); Heisler v. Thomas Colliery Co., 260 U.S. 245, 259, 260 (1922); Oliver Iron Co. v. Lord, 262 U.S. 172, 178 (1923); Champlin Refining Co. v. Corporation Commission, 286 U.S. 210, 235 (1932); Utah Power & Light Co. v. Pfost, 286 U.S. 165, 182 (1932); Chassaniol v. Greenwood, 291 U.S. 584, 587 (1934).

[25] Hammer v. Dagenhart, 247 U.S. 251 (1918).

ation a shipper who failed to comply with the regulation.[26]
It had also attempted, by the Grain Futures Act, regulation
of future trading in grain exchanges, again in the form of
prohibitory taxation upon those who failed to comply with
the regulations.[27] The Court struck down this attempt at
regulation on the ground that the activity was purely local.
The Court said:

"There is not a word in the Act from which it can be
gathered that it is confined in its operation to interstate commerce. . . A reading of the Act makes it quite clear that Congress sought to use the taxing power to give validity to the
Act. It did not have the exercise of its power under the commerce clause in mind and so did not introduce into the Act
the limitations which certainly would accompany and mark
an exercise of the power under the latter clause."

But at the same term—the October Term, 1921—the Court
sustained as a valid regulation of interstate commerce the
Packers and Stock Yards Act of 1921. This, like the Grain
Futures Act, attempted to regulate practices in areas which,
in a sense, were local, that is, areas in which the great stream
of livestock shipped from the West came to rest and was
converted into marketable meat for reshipment to various
sections of the country. In *Stafford* v. *Wallace*,[28] the Court
sustained this act as a regulation of commerce, because it
found from the proceedings of the committees in Congress
which had charge of the act, and from their reports, that the
purpose of the act was to remove a burden from interstate
commerce by regulating certain unfair practices which had
been found to limit competition and to burden that commerce.

At the following term, the Court was required to pass on
another act adopted by Congress in 1922 dealing with the

---

[26] Child Labor Tax Case, 259 U.S. 20 (1922).
[27] Hill v. Wallace, 259 U.S. 44 (1922).
[28] 258 U.S. 495 (1922).

grain futures business and intended to take the place of that held invalid in the prior year. This time the Court sustained the new act in *Board of Trade* v. *Olsen*.[29] Congress had supplied the lack which the Court found in the earlier act. In the title and in certain sections, the statute declared its purpose to be the prevention of obstructions and burdens upon interstate commerce in grain by regulating transactions on grain exchanges. Section 3 elaborated the rise and importance of the business and the fact that it was largely conducted in interstate commerce and that the subjects of the transactions largely moved in interstate commerce. The act declared that the obstructions and burdens upon interstate commerce in grain, consequent upon the practices of grain exchanges, rendered regulation imperative for the protection of interstate commerce. At the outset of its opinion, the Court distinguished its earlier decision in *Hill* v. *Wallace*,[30] stating that the act now before the Court contained the very features the absence of which was held in the earlier decision to condemn the legislation there considered. For the second time, the Court held that the transactions of a trader in commodities moving in interstate commerce, whose activities necessarily affected the flow of such commerce at a throat through which it passed, might be prospectively controlled by a federal system of statutory regulation.

These decisions opened a new field of regulation. Never before had Congress attempted to prevent interstate transportation of articles detrimental to health, or stolen articles, or kidnapped persons, either by a criminal statute purporting to punish the manufacture of such articles, the theft, or the kidnapping, or by a regulatory law covering local dealing in the states. But it was now established that where an activity was closely related to and affected the flow of commerce

---

[29] 262 U.S. 1 (1923).
[30] *Supra*, note 27.

from one state to another, the persons conducting such activity might be placed under federal regulation to be administered by a delegate of Congress. The question remained how far the principle could be carried.

In the national emergency arising at the close of the second decade of the twentieth century, Congress faced problems of depression in various industries, and it desired to deal with them on a national basis. The first comprehensive statute it adopted was the National Industrial Recovery Act, which provided for regulation of practices and prices, wholesale and retail, throughout the nation. An attempt was made to enforce the act against a small butchering concern in Brooklyn. The attempt was justified on the ground that the materials received by the defendant had passed to him through the channels of interstate commerce. It was held in *A.L.A. Schecter Corp.* v. *United States*[31] that the commerce had ceased when the butcher's activities began and that his practices in marketing his commodity could not be said to affect interstate commerce so as to be regulable by federal authority.

The plight of the country's farmers was thought to be a desperate one. In 1933, Congress passed the Agricultural Adjustment Act. The first section recited an emergency resulting from the disparity of prices of agricultural and other commodities, the diminution of the farmers' purchasing power, and a breakdown in exchange. The section continued to the effect that these things "burdened and obstructed the normal course of commerce, calling for legislation." The second section went on to say that the purpose of the act was to establish and maintain a balance between production and consumption of agricultural commodities, and to establish marketing conditions which would reëstablish farmers' prices and restore the farmers' purchasing power to that

[31] 295 U.S. 495 (1935); *cf.* Higgins v. Carr Brothers Co., 317 U.S. 572 (1943).

prevailing at an earlier date. The reduction of production of crops by farmers was to be induced by placing on processors of farm products a tax which would be earmarked for distribution among such farmers as would coöperate in a general scheme of allocation of farm production and price support.

This legislation was challenged in *United States* v. *Butler*.[32] The government disavowed any support for the statute under the commerce power. It relied solely on the taxing power as an instrument for promotion of general welfare. The exaction was held not to be a true tax and the scheme an endeavor to assess a given class for the benefit of another class. We need not further consider the case. It is cited only to show that whereas the preamble to the act indicated a purpose to relieve interstate commerce, this was not believed sufficient to validate its provisions.

The bituminous coal industry suffered severely in the depression of the early thirties. Congress was minded to afford relief both to the mine operators and to their employees. Now for the first time legislation was drafted with the idea of applying the doctrine of the *Shreveport Case* in reverse, if I may so phrase it. If the United States could nullify local intrastate action or activity, under state law, where it was contrary to a valid regulation of interstate commerce, why could it not envisage future and threatened injury to and burden on interstate commerce by existing or potential local activity and, in order to avoid prospective injury to that commerce, proceed to regiment and regulate the conduct of local business? On the theory that it could do so, Congress passed the Bituminous Coal Conservation Act of 1935.

This act placed on the production of bituminous coal a tax, which was to be reduced in the case of those producers who agreed to enter into price-fixing agreements; it also set up a Board to enforce certain labor policies and to regulate labor

[32] 297 U.S. 1 (1936).

relations at the mines. The act was attacked and was held invalid by a divided court in *Carter* v. *Carter Coal Co.*[33] This was the first act which purported to state in detail reasons for its enactment, based on the commerce power. Section 1 declared that the production and distribution of bituminous coal bear upon and directly affect interstate commerce and render regulation of production and distribution imperative for the protection of such commerce. It added that the practices of the industry tend to the disorganization of interstate commerce in coal and tend to burden and obstruct that commerce; that prevailing practices in coal production directly affect interstate commerce and require regulation for the protection of such commerce; that the right of mine workers to organize and bargain collectively should be guaranteed in order to prevent wage cutting and disparate labor costs detrimental to fair interstate competition and to avoid obstruction to interstate commerce owing to labor disputes. Thus the attempt was to enter the local field of production and regulate it as a means of lifting burdens from the ensuing commerce in the commodity locally produced.

The effort failed. The Court followed its earlier decisions to the effect that the local production of coal was not interstate commerce and could not be regulated as such. It disposed of the contention that the practices attempted to be remedied burdened interstate commerce by asserting that any burden which existed was indirect; and that, if Congress had power to reach indirect burdens on commerce, it would be difficult to say that any local practice by one or many citizens did not ultimately have some effect on commerce, and impossible to set any limit to the things Congress might regulate in the guise of fostering or protecting interstate commerce.

The Chief Justice, who dissented in part, agreed that the

[33] 298 U.S. 238 (1936).

labor provisions of the act were invalid, but thought that the statute was severable, and that the provisions regarding prices might be sustained as a regulation of prices charged in interstate transactions. He said:

"But Congress may not use this protective authority as a pretext for the exercise of power to regulate activities and relations within the states which affect interstate commerce only indirectly. Otherwise, in view of the magnitude of indirect effects, Congress in its discretion could assume control of virtually all the activities of the people to the subversion of the fundamental principle of the Constitution."

Two other dissenting justices held the act severable and the price provisions appropriate regulations of interstate commerce, but refused to pass upon the labor provisions in the posture in which the case stood before the Court.

This decision was the high-water mark of the doctrine that Congress cannot regulate local activities. The opinion definitely rejects the magnitude of the local operations as a material factor. The Court makes the test one of directness, as against remoteness. Whether the decision is sound or the reverse, the Court was surely right in saying that a contrary decision would open the door to federal regulation of local activities to an almost unlimited extent.

Two years later the *Carter* case, with the line of decisions on which it relied, was so limited as to be virtually overruled. In 1935, Congress addressed itself to the general problems of labor relations. For years the country had been plagued by labor controversies. Statutes and decisions in the various states differed widely, and it was thought that a uniform system of regulation of labor relations would aid in the solution of the problem. Union recognition and collective bargaining had been strongly advocated. The question arose whether Congress could establish a uniform system for the whole nation. Addressing itself to the problem, Congress adopted the National Labor Relations Act. It was thought necessary to spell out the relation of the proposed legislation to the power to regulate interstate commerce. This was done by a preamble or declaration of purpose intended to show that what Congress was hitting at was the burden and obstruction to interstate commerce which resulted from strikes, inequality of bargaining power of labor, and other incidents of the employer–employee relation. It seems worth while to quote the first section of the act in full. It is:

"Section 1. The denial by employers of the right of employees to organize and the refusal of employers to accept the procedure of collective bargaining lead to strikes and other forms of industrial strife or unrest, which have the intent or the necessary effect of burdening or obstructing commerce by (a) impairing the efficiency, safety, or operation of the instrumentalities of commerce; (b) occurring in the current of commerce; (c) materially affecting, restraining, or controlling the flow of raw materials or manufactured or processed goods from or into the channels of commerce, or the prices of such materials or goods in commerce; or (d) causing diminution of employment and wages in such volume as substantially to impair or disrupt the market for goods flowing from or into the channels of commerce.

"The inequality of bargaining power between employees who do not possess full freedom of association or actual liberty of contract, and employers who are organized in the corporate or other forms of ownership association substantially burdens and affects the flow of commerce, and tends to aggravate recurrent business depressions, by depressing wage rates and the purchasing power of wage earners in industry and by preventing the stabilization of competitive wage rates and working conditions within and between industries.

"Experience has proved that protection by law of the right

of employees to organize and bargain collectively safeguards commerce from injury, impairment, or interruption, and promotes the flow of commerce by removing certain recognized sources of industrial strife and unrest, by encouraging practices fundamental to the friendly adjustment of industrial disputes arising out of differences as to wages, hours, or other working conditions, and by restoring equality of bargaining power between employers and employees.

"It is hereby declared to be the policy of the United States to eliminate the cause of certain substantial obstructions to the free flow of commerce and to mitigate and eliminate these obstructions when they have occurred by encouraging the practice and procedure of collective bargaining and by protecting the exercise by workers of full freedom of association, self-organization, and designation of representatives of their own choosing, for the purpose of negotiating the terms and conditions of their employment or other mutual aid or protection."

On the footing of this declaration, Congress defined commerce in classical terms and defined acts affecting commerce. It established a Board to administer the law. It declared the right of employees to self-organization and to bargain collectively through their chosen representatives; it defined unfair labor practices; it specified how employees should be represented in collective bargaining; it empowered the Board to correct the defined unfair labor practices, and set up a procedure to be followed by the Board. It made the Board's findings of fact, if supported by evidence, conclusive, and gave a limited court review of Board action.

The first case challenging the statute was *Labor Board* v. *Jones & Laughlin Steel Corp.*[34] The Board, after a hearing and findings based thereon, had entered an order upon the complaint of a labor union finding the respondent guilty of

[34] 301 U.S. 1 (1937).

unfair labor practices within the meaning of the statute. The respondent contested the order on the ground that the act was in reality a regulation of labor relations rather than of interstate commerce, and that the respondent's relations with the employees engaged in production of steel were not subject to regulation by the federal goverment. These contentions were overruled.

The Court approved the definition of the phrase "affecting commerce" embodied in the statute. This the statute says "means in commerce or burdening or obstructing commerce, or the free flow of commerce, or having led or tending to lead to a labor dispute burdening or obstructing commerce or the free flow of commerce." The Court pointed out that the statute does not purport to give authority to the Board over relationship between all industrial employees and employers, but that it purports to reach only what may be deemed to burden or obstruct interstate commerce. The Court felt, therefore, that it must examine whether the alleged unfair labor practices might burden or obstruct such commerce. After citing the earlier declarations of the Court that manufacturing is not commerce, it concluded that it is not beyond reason that industrial disputes in an establishment such as that conducted by the respondent would have an adverse effect on interstate commerce. The Court said:

"Giving full weight to respondent's contention with respect to a break in the complete continuity of the 'stream of commerce' by reason of respondent's manufacturing operations, the fact remains that the stoppage of those operations by industrial strife would have a most serious effect upon interstate commerce. In view of respondent's far-flung activities, it is idle to state that the effect would be indirect or remote. It is obvious that it would be immediate and might be catastrophic."

This, of course, was said of one of the largest industries in a vital field of production. But, as a basis of decision, it was in the teeth of what the *Carter* opinion declared, that is, that the magnitude of the local operation was immaterial. However, the Court did not reserve to itself the function of appraising the extent of the alleged burden on commerce in any given case.

In subsequent adjudications, the Court felt itself bound by the findings of the Board as to the effect of the activities of the smallest operations upon commerce. In no case did the Court essay to override the Board's conclusion that the effect on commerce of a condemned labor practice was a forbidden burden on interstate commerce. Once the bridge of power was crossed, had it any alternative? The Board spoke on a question of fact as the *alter ego*, the accredited organ of the legislature. Were its findings any less binding than if they had been made by Congress itself? If the test was no longer that of direct interference or burden, it became one of limits, and how could a court say that the legislative judgment as to the burdensome effect of a given practice, though the Court might have reached a different conclusion, was wrong as a matter of law? The *Carter* case had retained the question of "directness" as a justiciable one. That test was abandoned. The opinion states: "In the *Carter Case*, the Court was of the opinion that the provisions of the statute relating to production were invalid upon several grounds,—that there was improper delegation of legislative power, and that the requirements not only went beyond any sustainable measure of protection of interstate commerce, but were also inconsistent with due process. *These cases* [Carter and others] *are not controlling here*."[35]

The same technique as that of the National Labor Relations

[35] Italics supplied. The *Carter* case was to all intents overruled in United States v. Darby, 312 U.S. 100, 123 (1941).

Act was used in a number of statutes passed about the same time. Each provided regulation of a local activity for the asserted purpose of protecting interstate commerce. Among them were the Agricultural Marketing Act of 1938 and the Fair Labor Standards Act of 1938. The first was intended to accomplish the same purpose as the earlier legislation condemned in *United States* v. *Butler*.[36] This time, however, the regulation of farming was planted squarely on the protection of interstate commerce. In *Mulford* v. *Smith*,[37] the act's provisions for controlling the raising of tobacco were sustained in view of the declared purpose.[38] And in *Wickard* v. *Filburn*,[39] the provisions regarding wheat were sustained to the extent of holding that to penalize a farmer for storing and feeding to his cattle wheat in excess of the quantity he was permitted to produce was necessary to the plan of the act to protect interstate commerce.

In 1938 Congress entered still another field in the Fair Labor Standards Act, which withstood attack in *United States* v. *Darby*.[40] In this legislation the new technique was again adopted to justify regulation of hours of labor and wages in local industry, such as mining and manufacturing. Section 2 declares:

"The Congress hereby finds that the existence, in industries engaged in commerce or in the production of goods for commerce, of labor conditions detrimental to the maintenance of the minimum standard of living necessary for health, efficiency, and general well-being of workers (1) causes commerce and the channels and instrumentalities of commerce to be

[36] *Supra*, note 32.
[37] 307 U.S. 38 (1939).
[38] See the statement of purpose, 307 U.S. 38, at 41, 42.
[39] 317 U.S. 111 (1942). In United States v. Rock Royal Co-operative, 307 U.S. 533 (1939), and United States v. Wrightwood Dairy Co., 315 U.S. 110 (1942), regulation of production and interstate marketing of milk under the Agricultural Marketing Agreements Act of 1939 were sustained.
[40] 312 U.S. 100 (1941).

used to spread and perpetuate such labor conditions among the workers of the several States; (2) burdens commerce and the free flow of goods in commerce; (3) constitutes an unfair method of competition in commerce; (4) leads to labor disputes burdening and obstructing commerce and the free flow of goods in commerce; and (5) interferes with the orderly and fair marketing of goods in commerce."

The act fixed minimum wages and maximum hours of labor for employees engaged in interstate commerce or in "the production of goods" for such commerce. It made it a crime for an employer to violate the act in his employment or to fail to keep records of the work-time and wages of the persons he employs. The form of such records was to be prescribed by a federal administrator. The indictment in the *Darby* case charged a violation by one whose business was sawing logs into lumber with the intent to ship the lumber in interstate commerce, and did so ship a large part of it. There was a demurrer on the ground that the act unconstitutionally sought to regulate a local business which the state of domicile had not seen fit to regulate.

Mr. Justice Stone, in writing the opinion of the Court, traced in detail the growth of legislation and the extension of the areas covered by it over the years. In the light of this history, he first considered that phase of the act which prohibited the shipment in interstate commerce of goods manufactured under local conditions condemned by statute. The opinion showed that the Court had been unwilling to examine the motive or purpose of legislation excluding commodities from interstate shipment, and declared *Hammer* v. *Dagenhart*[41] to be out of line with the Court's subsequent adjudications, and overruled it. This brought Mr. Justice Stone to a consideration of the wages and hours requirements of the act. The opinion, after tracing the development of the regula-

[41] *Supra*, note 25.

tion of activities believed to burden commerce, which I have earlier described, notes the extension that was made in previous doctrine when the National Labor Relations Act was sustained. The opinion shows that the trend of the decisions in this field in effect precludes the Court's saying that in its judgment Congress could not regulate under the commerce clause the wages and the hours of labor of persons whose work was in commerce or who produced goods for commerce.

Of course, the effect of sustaining the act was to place the whole matter of wages and hours of persons employed throughout the United States, with slight exceptions, under a single federal regulatory scheme and in this way completely to supersede state exercise of the police power in this field.

As has usually been true, once the power of Congress in the premises was conceded, it became difficult for the Court to limit the legislative exercise of that power, however sweeping. In this instance no administrative body was constituted to examine the facts and issue orders, such as the Interstate Commerce Commission or the National Labor Relations Board. Here enforcement was left to litigation instituted by the government. The Court might have scrutinized individual cases and found in some of them that the connection of a person's work with interstate commerce was indirect, remote, or incidental, and that an attempt to regulate his wages and hours was, therefore, beyond the power of Congress. On the contrary, the Court has interpreted the act broadly and has held it applicable to extreme cases. Indeed, the opinions turn rather on the meaning of the words "produced for commerce" than on the effect of the conditions of work on commerce. Thus, in *Warren-Bradshaw Drilling Co.* v. *Hall*,[42] the statute was held to apply to the wages and hours of a member of a drilling crew employed by an independent con-

[42] 317 U.S. 88 (1942).

tractor in the partial drilling of oil wells. These wells, it was shown, did not reach the producing sands during the performance of the contract, but were afterwards completed and some oil and gas from them moved in interstate commerce. It was held that the act covered the case.

In *Overstreet* v. *North Shore Corp.*,[43] the attendants on a drawbridge over which automobiles passed in interstate travel were held to be within the act; as was, in *Walton* v. *Southern Package Corp.*,[44] a night watchman in a manufacturing plant, which shipped a substantial portion of its product in interstate commerce. In *Borden* v. *Borella*,[45] maintenance men working in an office building owned by a company which produced goods for commerce, used about one half the space for its executives, and rented the balance to strangers, were held within the act. On the other hand, in *10 E. 40th Street* v. *Callus*,[46] similar maintenance employees of an office building in a large city which rented all the space in the building to tenants indifferently, some of the tenants' business being the production of goods for commerce, were held by the Court, by the narrowest of margins, to be not within the act. And in *Higgins* v. *Carr Brothers Co.*,[47] an employee in a wholesale house who worked on goods received in interstate commerce after such receipt, the goods then being sold in intrastate commerce, was held not within the act's coverage. In *McLeod* v. *Threlkeld*,[48] a cook for a railroad maintenance-of-way crew was held neither in commerce nor producing goods for commerce.

Be it noted, however, that only the meaning of the act was decided. The cases are not concerned with any question of excessive assertion of the power of Congress.

It will be seen that in recent years, by virtue of the exer-

[43] 318 U.S. 125 (1943).
[44] 320 U.S. 540 (1944).
[45] 325 U.S. 679 (1945).
[46] 325 U.S. 578 (1945).
[47] 317 U.S. 572 (1943).
[48] 319 U.S. 491 (1943).

cise of the commerce power to remove prospective burdens on interstate commerce arising out of purely local practices and conditions, the Congress has superseded the police power of the states and taken unto itself police power in a vast field of business and other activity. Under the Agricultural Acts, the practices and production of farmers are regulated; under the Securities Exchange Act, brokers and sellers of securities are regulated; under the National Labor Relations Act, producers, manufacturers, and processors are brought under regulatory control; and under the Fair Labor Standards Act, the regulation of nearly all wages and hours of workers the country over is imposed.

It seems pretty hard to draw a line in respect of this type of federal prophylactic legislation. Its operation must be permitted to extend to the smallest units and to activities that once were thought so remote from interstate commerce as to have no appreciable effect on it. In the light of these decisions, it is hard to think of any local business which Congress may not regulate if it professes to believe that the operations of that business may be detrimental, in however slight or remote a degree, to interstate commerce.

In my opening lecture, I discussed the taxing power, but I have thought it appropriate to postpone to this context an exercise of that power which seems to me to be supplementary to what has been done under the aegis of the commerce power, which covers a field that probably could not be reached under the commerce power. It has long been held that if a government so elected, it might regulate the activities of citizens indirectly by use of the taxing power. I have already shown that legislation by Congress intended to drive out of existence bank issues thought to be inimical to the fiscal operations of the federal government were sustained in *Veazie Bank* v. *Fenno*.[49] It would seem clear that,

[49] 8 Wall. 533 (1869).

if Congress has power to regulate an activity, it has power to regulate it through channels of taxation.[50] But, at times Congress attempted to penalize by a tax on interstate shipment the product of condemned local activity. This it did in an endeavor to prevent child labor in industry. At the time, *Hammer* v. *Dagenhart*[51] still represented the law. Under the force of that decision, Congress was incompetent to regulate conditions of labor in local industries. Applying the principle, the Court held in the *Child Labor Tax Case*[52] that Congress could not do so indirectly by penalizing in the form of a tax the product of such industry which passed into interstate commerce.

Many years later Congress adopted a different approach. In the Social Security Act of 1935, it inserted certain chapters dealing with unemployment compensation, child welfare, and other similar matters which had traditionally been concerns of the states rather than of the national government. One chapter of the statute laid a heavy excise tax on the privilege of employing persons to work for the taxpayer. This was a straight excise tax. The moneys collected were to go into the United States Treasury without identification or segregation. They became general funds of the United States. In a separate chapter, it was provided that any taxpayer who contributed to an approved state unemployment compensation fund should be credited up to 90 per cent of the tax he would otherwise be obliged to pay. I shall not go into detail with regard to the regulatory provisions concerning such state funds. Suffice it to say that no such fund could be approved by federal authority for tax deduction purposes unless it met certain standards and received the approval of a federal bureau. The act also provided that such state funds must make the United States Treasury the depositary of

[50] See Sunshine Anthracite Coal Co. v. Adkins, 310 U.S. 381 (1940).
[51] *Supra,* note 25.
[52] 259 U. S. 20 (1922).

their moneys and would have from time to time to withdraw these moneys from the Treasury under regulations promulgated by a federal board. As a separate provision, the act appropriated large sums to assist such state funds as by compliance with the requirements of the act obtained approval of the federal board.

In *Steward Machine Co. v. Davis*,[53] an employer whose state maintained no such state unemployment fund attacked the act as in excess of Congressional power, as an invasion of the states' rights under the Tenth Amendment, and for other reasons. The act was sustained. It was held to be merely an effort on the part of Congress to aid such states as might voluntarily desire such aid. It was said that coöperation between federal and state governments was beneficial; that so long as the states were free to elect whether they would coöperate on the basis specified by Congress, there was no undue compulsion or pressure upon them and no reason why the action of Congress should not be construed as for the general welfare, for which that body had an undoubted right to appropriate. The Court negatived the contention that the excise tax was a mere oppressive instrument intended to force states and the citizens of states to come into one general uniform system of unemployment compensation controlled by the United States. It said that on the face of the statute the tax was an excise and nothing more; that the moneys raised by that excise were the general moneys of the United States not devoted to any scheme or plan of unemployment compensation; that the proffer of coöperation and assistance to the states was made in the exercise of the welfare powers of Congress; and that its support would come from the general moneys of the United States and was in no sense tied in with the taxing provision so as to make that provision a club held over local governments or their citizens.

[53] 301 U.S. 548 (1937).

The Social Security Act also provided for financial assistance to the states in the fields of aid to dependent children, maternal care and child welfare, public health and aid to the blind. All of this was on the same pattern as the provisions for unemployment compensation. The assistance could only be obtained and continued by compliance with standards fixed by the federal government.

When we add this type of federal legislation to that which Congress may enact under the commerce power, it becomes apparent that if Congress so determines, not only local business activities but local social and community services may be taken from the states and, in effect, assumed by the federal government. The process may not be coercion. It may be that the courts cannot adjudge that the general appropriation of financial aid to the states is not for the "general welfare." But it remains that if the appropriation is conditioned on compliance by the states with federally established standards and with the orders of a federal administrator, and if it be required that a state deposit its funds in the federal Treasury, there is little autonomy left.

Taxes are of myriad forms. Ingenuity can probably bring forth some form of excise, such as that in the Social Security Act, that will make it very expensive to live in a state which does not enter the federal aid system.

The continual expansion of federal power with consequent contraction of state powers probably has been inevitable. The founders of the Republic envisaged no such economic and other expansion as the nation has experienced. Looking back, it is difficult to see how the Court could have resisted the popular urge for uniform standards throughout the country—for what in effect was a unified economy. It may be that in a sense the resort of Congress to the taxing power, to the general welfare power, and to the commerce power as means to reach a result never contemplated when the Constitution was adopted, was a subterfuge. An insistence by the Court on holding federal power to what seemed its appropriate orbit when the Constitution was adopted might have resulted in even more radical changes in our dual structure than those which have been gradually accomplished through the extension of the limited jurisdiction conferred on the federal government.

I have adverted to the fact that the Court has acted to circumscribe the police power of the states on the ground that attempted exercise of that power trenched upon the domain of Congress under the commerce power—this in the absence of any Congressional declaration of federal policy. I have also noted that, in extreme cases, the Court has felt compelled to decide that Congress has exceeded its delegated powers in attempting to reach state concerns. The deference which the Court rightly shows to the propriety of action by a coördinate branch of the government has usually constrained the Court to yield what its own views might have been to those expressed by the Congress concerning the necessity and the reach of federal power.

There is no doubt that the Supreme Court remains the final arbiter between the state and nation. Doubtless extreme cases will in the future, as they have in the past, call for an exertion of the Court's ultimate authority. In *McCray* v. *United States*,[54] the Court said that if a case were presented where the abuse of the taxing power was so extreme that it was "plain to the judicial mind that the power had been called into play not for revenue but solely for the purpose of destroying rights which could not be rightfully destroyed consistently with the principles of freedom and justice upon which the Constitution rests, that it would be the duty of the courts to say that such an arbitrary act was not merely an

[54] 195 U.S. 27, 64 (1904).

abuse of a delegated power but was the exercise of an authority not conferred."

The same no doubt is true of the commerce power. In *Carolene Products Co.* v. *United States*,[55] it was said that when Congress exercises a delegated power such as the commerce power, the methods it employs may be stricken down only upon a clear and convincing showing that there is no rational basis for the legislation. But, in the light of our growing solidarity as a nation, and in the light of the pressures, wise or not, for uniform regulation in various fields, the Congress has felt constrained to stretch its granted powers to the utmost and to treat as corollaries of those powers manifestations of police power which tend to reduce the states to administrative districts rather than coördinate sovereigns; and, in the main, the Supreme Court has felt constrained to give full faith and credit to the legislature's declared purpose to exercise, not to transcend, the powers granted it.

[55] 323 U.S. 18 (1944).

III. The Fourteenth Amendment

I wish now to discuss the role of the Supreme Court in the application of the Fourteenth Amendment in order to lead up to my conclusions. These are that the Court's decisions represent an alternation between expansion of federal power not expressly conferred and an effort to protect state sovereignty.

For the sake of background, I shall restate some trite propositions. First, Amendments I to VIII inclusive are limitations not upon the exercise of power by the states, but upon exercise of it by the United States. The history of these amendments, the form of their statement, and the subjects with which they deal are convincing evidence of this. There has been no difference of opinion on the point.[1] On only one occasion prior to the Civil War did the Court fully discuss the due process clause of the Fifth Amendment. In *Murray's Lessee v. Hoboken Land and Improvement Co.*,[2] a question arose as to the title to real estate acquired at a United States Marshal's sale pursuant to a distress warrant issued by the Solicitor of the United States Treasury. A federal statute provided for the issue of such distress warrants against customs officials for any debit balance in their accounts. No question was raised regarding the regularity of the warrant, its proper entry in

---

[1] Barron v. Baltimore, 7 Pet. 243 (1833); Livingston v. Moore, 7 Pet. 469 (1833); United States v. Cruikshank, 92 U.S. 542 (1876).
[2] 18 How. 272 (1856).

the Federal District Court, or any of the proceedings leading to the marshal's sale. These steps were all in accordance with the statute.

The question presented was whether the due process clause of the Fifth Amendment forbade such a summary proceeding for the collection of moneys due the United States by one of its officers. The Court remarked that the words "due process of law" were undoubtedly intended to convey the same meaning as the words "by the law of the land" used in the Magna Charta. After calling attention to the fact that the Constitution provides for the trial of all crimes, except cases of impeachment, by jury, and that by the Sixth and Seventh Amendments further special provisions were made for jury trial in civil and criminal cases, the Court concluded that to have used the words of the Magna Charta, that is, that no person shall be deprived of his life, liberty, or property but by the judgment of his peers or the law of the land, would have been in part superfluous and tautological. The Court then sought to find a meaning which could be assigned to the phrase "due process of law" in consonance with the other constitutional provisions. This the Court did, first by examining the Constitution to ascertain whether the process used in the instant case was in conflict with any other provision of that instrument. It was found not to be. The Court then proceeded to a second inquiry, namely, whether the proceeding was consistent with "those several usages and improvements of proceedings existing in the common and statute law of England before the emigration of our ancestors which are not unsuited to their civil and political conditions because acted on by them subsequent to the settlement of this country." The opinion then demonstrated that in England it was accepted practice for the Crown to collect duties due it by such summary proceeding and that, in some of the colonies and the states, the same procedure had been followed. It noted that in the instant case, the steps required by the statute had been followed, but said that if Congress, in enacting the statute, had transgressed the constitutional guaranty, the mere fact that the procedure was regular would not save the statute. This was but to say that none of the departments of government is free from the compulsion of the amendment.

After the Civil War the Congress adopted three amendments which, as we know, were primarily directed to the protection of the emancipated negro population. The Thirteenth abolished human slavery. The Fifteenth forbade denial or abridgment, by nation or state, of the right of citizens to vote on account of race, color, or previous condition of servitude. The Fourteenth, with which we are concerned, consisted of five sections. Only the first and fifth are material to the present discussion.

The first section embodies a declaration and three prohibitions. The opening sentence declares that all persons born or naturalized in the United States and subject to the jurisdiction thereof are citizens of the United States and of the state wherein they reside. This declaration was intended to set at rest the doubts which had been raised by the *Dred Scott* case,[3] whether a citizen of the United States must be recognized by a state as its citizen. The three clauses of the second sentence provide that no state shall make or enforce any law which shall abridge the privileges or immunities of citizens of the United States; nor shall any state deprive any person of life, liberty, or property, without due process of law; nor deny to any person within its jurisdiction the equal protection of the laws.

It is interesting to observe in how few cases the Supreme Court has enforced the first and third clauses against state

[3] Scott v. Sandford, 19 How. 393 (1857).

action, as compared with the great number of cases decided under the due process clause. It is not within my purpose to deal with this matter in detail, but it is worthy of remark that, in contrast to the due process clause, the privileges and immunities clause and the equal protection clause have been held to a very narrow content. The first mentioned has been found to apply only to rights obviously belonging to citizens of the United States as such, for instance, the right to petition Congress for a redress of grievances, to vote for national officers, to enter public lands, to inform the United States authorities of violation of its laws.[4]

The equal protection clause has largely been limited in application to discrimination on account of race or color.[5] A host of claims of denial of equal protection has been answered by the Court's sustaining the right of the state to classify, for the purposes of taxation, or regulation, or to exempt persons or classes from the application of a general statute. Comparatively few claims under this clause have been sustained.

The great mass of constitutional litigation arising under the Fourteenth Amendment has fallen under the due process clause. A fair reading of the clause should seem to indicate that the word "person" as used in that clause refers to natural persons. The first sentence of the section speaks of all persons born or naturalized. The first clause of the second sentence refers to citizens of the United States. The due process and equal protection clauses each refer to any person, and the former protects the life, liberty, or property of such person. A corporation is not born or naturalized and is not a citizen of the United States. A corporation has only in a metaphorical sense a life of which it might be deprived. Nevertheless, the Court has held that a corporation is a person

[4] Twining v. New Jersey, 211 U.S. 78, 97 (1908).

[5] Strauder v. West Virginia, 100 U.S. 303 (1880); Norris v. Alabama, 294 U.S. 587 (1935); Nixon v. Herndon, 273 U.S. 536 (1927).

within the meaning of the due process clause[6] and within the meaning of the equal protection clause.[7] On the other hand, a corporation has been held not to be a citizen within the privileges and immunities clause.[8]

Likewise, liberty has been given a broad connotation. Witness the unfortunate decisions as to liberty of contract of which *Coppage* v. *Kansas*[9] is typical. But, after all, these were constructions of the meaning of the terms.

A very different problem was presented by the necessity to give definition to the prohibition against deprivation of life, liberty, or property without due process of law. At first, the Court proceeded with caution, pursuing a policy of exclusion rather than of inclusion, endeavoring to find that state action, for one reason or another, did not offend the guaranty. But gradually it came to be held that the phrase had a broader sweep than was given it in *Murray's Lessee* v. *Hoboken Land and Improvement Co.*[10] State action, regarding which neither of the tests used in that case was apposite, was condemned for arbitrariness, for lack of fairness assumed to be a postulate of the sort of civilized society for which our government exists. Soon the question arose whether the Fourteenth Amendment was intended to make applicable to the states all the guaranties of the first eight amendments.

The Court sternly refused to hold that the privileges and immunities clause had that effect; and in this view it has persisted. That clause, be it remarked, might with much greater

---

[6] Covington & Turnpike Road Co. v. Sandford, 164 U.S. 578 (1896); Grosjean v. American Press Co., 297 U.S. 233, 244 (1936); see the views of Mr. Justice Black dissenting in Connecticut General Life Ins. Co. v. Johnson, 303 U.S. 77, 83 (1938).

[7] Smyth v. Ames, 169 U.S. 466 (1898); Liggett Co. v. Baldridge, 278 U.S. 105 (1928).

[8] Paul v. Virginia, 8 Wall. 168 (1869); Grosjean v. American Press Co., *supra*, note 6.

[9] 236 U.S. 1 (1915).

[10] *Supra*, note 2.

reason than the due process clause have been held so to
operate.

Prior to the adoption of the Fourteenth Amendment, it had
been held in *Barron* v. *Baltimore*[11] that the clause of the
Fifth Amendment which requires just compensation for property taken for public use has no application to the states.

Less than ten years after adoption of the Fourteenth, the
Court decided *Davidson* v. *New Orleans*.[12] This is what the
Court said on the question whether the due process clause
embodied the principle of just compensation expressly stated
in the Fifth: "If private property be taken for public uses
without just compensation, it must be remembered that, when
the Fourteenth Amendment was adopted, the provision on
that subject, in immediate juxtaposition in the Fifth Amendment with the one we are construing, was left out, and this
[the due process clause] was taken."

In 1896, thirty years after the adoption of the Fourteenth
Amendment, Mr. Justice Harlan, speaking for a unanimous
Court, declared in *Chicago, Burlington and Quincy R.R.* v.
Chicago[13] that if a state attempted to take private property
for public use without making just compensation therefor,
this action would be a violation of due process of law as
guaranteed in the amendment. The opinion contains quite a
discussion of the concept of due process of law, but says not
a word about the fact that, in the Fifth Amendment—and in
the very same sentence in which the due process clause
occurs—the duty to make such compensation is stated as a
separate guaranty against action by the United States. Thus,
without discussion of the history of the doctrine of due
process in the light of Anglo-Saxon tradition concerning the
power of the Crown to expropriate lands for public use, or
the reason why the framers of the Fifth Amendment felt
it necessary, in addition to the due process clause, to insert

[11] *Supra*, note 1.   [12] 96 U.S. 97 (1878).   [13] 166 U.S. 226 (1897).

a clause covering the matter of just compensation for property taken for public use, the opinion reaches the conclusion that the concept of due process embraces the obligation of the sovereign to make compensation for property taken.

In quick succession the ruling was repeated, Mr. Justice Harlan speaking for the Court in each case and always in a brief statement without explication or elaboration.[14] It is interesting to observe that, in the first case which announced the doctrine, the constitution of the State of Illinois contained a provision for just compensation for property taken for public use; that the railroad's property was taken pursuant to a statute which provided for a trial on the question of the amount of compensation to be awarded; that, as a result of such trial, a jury awarded one dollar compensation; that the Supreme Court insisted that, if the proceeding resulted in an unjust award, which the Supreme Court of Illinois had sustained, the Supreme Court was bound to reëxamine the case since the action of the state court was state action within the meaning of the Fourteenth Amendment; and that, after such examination, the Court sustained the jury's verdict and the judgment entered thereon.

It is also interesting that in *Smyth* v. *Ames*,[15] Mr. Justice Harlan quoted from *Reagan* v. *Farmers' Loan and Trust Co.*, 154 U.S. 362 (1894), the following:

"In every Constitution is the guaranty against the taking of private property for public use without just compensation. The equal protection of the laws which by the Fourteenth Amendment no State can deny to the individual, forbids legislation, in whatever form it may be enacted, by which the property of one individual is, without compensation, wrested from him for the benefit of another, or of the public."

[14] Smyth v. Ames, 169 U.S. 466, 524 (1898); Norwood v. Baker, 172 U.S. 269, 277 (1898); San Diego Land and Town Co. v. National City, 174 U.S. 739, 754 (1899).

[15] *Supra*, note 7.

It will thus be seen that the Court seemed quite indifferent whether to place the protection in question under the due process or the equal protection clause. With so little discussion and analysis of the ground of decision, the first inclination to read into the due process clause something contained in one of the early amendments of the Constitution came to fruition.

The Fourteenth Amendment had been a part of the Constitution for over fifty years, when the Court first suggested that freedom of speech and of the press are among the personal rights and liberties protected by the due process clause from impairment by the states.

In *Gitlow* v. *New York*,[16] a state statute was drawn in question which defined criminal anarchy and advocacy of criminal anarchy, whether by word of mouth or by writing, and punished such advocacy. In a prosecution for violation of this law, the defendant was convicted and his conviction was sustained by the highest court of the state. Upon appeal, the Supreme Court, Mr. Justice Holmes and Mr. Justice Brandeis dissenting, affirmed the conviction. The pivot of the case was whether the defendant's conduct was such as to create a clear and present danger that it would bring about substantive evils that a state has a right to prevent. The clear and present danger test had been applied in cases arising under federal law where the First Amendment had been invoked against the application of the statute to alleged violators.[17]

Mr. Justice Brandeis, in his dissenting opinion, said:

"The general principle of free speech, it seems to me, must be taken to be included in the Fourteenth Amendment, in view of the scope that has been given to the word 'liberty' as there used, although perhaps it may be accepted with a

[16] 268 U.S. 652 (1925).
[17] Schenck v. United States, 249 U.S. 47 (1919); Abrams v. United States, 250 U.S. 616 (1919).

somewhat larger latitude of interpretation than is allowed to Congress by the sweeping language that governs or ought to govern the laws of the United States."

In the majority opinion, it was said:

"For present purposes we may and do assume that freedom of speech and of the press which are protected by the First Amendment from abridgment by Congress are among the fundamental personal rights and 'liberties' protected by the due process clause of the Fourteenth Amendment from impairment by the States."

That which the dissent asserted, and the majority opinion assumed, has become settled doctrine in the Court.[18]

The inclusion of the just compensation clause of the Fifth Amendment in the sweep of the Fourteenth was a strong exercise of the judicial power, notwithstanding that most state constitutions included a similar guarantee of compensation. It made possible a review of all rate litigation by states, which would otherwise have terminated in state courts.

But that extension was mild compared with the decision that the liberties protected by the due process clause included those to be implied from the provisions of the First Amendment. This decision was the most sweeping judicial extension of federal power over state action in the history of the republic. The result is not implicit in the language of the due process clause any more than is the doctrine that the sovereign must pay for what he takes. Various explanations have been offered in support of the decision. One of these is that, though the Fourteenth Amendment does not say so, its legislative history is convincing that it was intended to draw in and make applicable to the states all the provisions of the first eight amendments. This is the view advocated

[18] Stromberg v. California, 283 U.S. 359, 368 (1931); Near v. Minnesota, 283 U.S. 697 (1931); Grosjean v. American Press Co., 297 U.S. 233, 243 (1936).

by Mr. Justice Black.[19] It seems to me a much stronger case against such reading of the legislative history is made by Charles Fairman in his recent examination of the subject.[20]

I suggest that the propriety of the Court's action in attributing to the due process clause a purpose to embody the guaranties of the early amendments is better determined by an examination of the writings themselves. First to be noted is that the language used in the Fifth is the same as that employed in the Fourteenth. The Fifth reads: "nor shall any person . . . be deprived of life, liberty, or property, without due process of law." The Fourteenth states: "nor shall any State deprive any person of life, liberty, or property, without due process of law." The meaning of the words used in the two amendments must be the same; and so it has uniformly been held. For the most part, the original interpretations were of the phrase of the Fourteenth Amendment; and later there developed an extensive effort to apply against the United States the same principles announced by the Court as applicable to the states under the Fourteenth. The Court's interpretation of the language of the due process clause of the Fifth Amendment has followed, not preceded, that adopted concerning the same clause of the Fourteenth.

It seems a fair method of testing the theory that the due process clause draws in the first eight amendments to endeavor to ascertain what was intended to be covered by the due process clause of the Fifth. I should like first to examine the whole text of the Fifth Amendment with this in mind. The first clause forbids holding a person to answer for a capital or infamous crime unless on a presentment or indictment by a grand jury, with a saving clause concerning cases arising in the land or naval forces, or in the militia in actual service

[19] Adamson v. California, 332 U.S. 46 (1947); *cf.* Wolf v. Colorado, 338 U.S. 25 (1949).
[20] 2 STANFORD LAW REVIEW 5 (December 1949).

in time of war or public danger. It seems evident that this clause recognized that other methods of holding a person to answer for crime might be within the traditions of the common law and of our states, and that the clause was adopted for the purpose of showing that no other form of accusation, whether traditional or not, was to be used by the federal government in the case of serious offenses.

The next clause forbids that any person be twice put in jeopardy for the same offense. The next forbids that any person be compelled to be a witness against himself in a criminal case. Then comes the due process clause. The amendment concludes with a prohibition against the taking of private property for public use without just compensation. As used in the Fifth Amendment, therefore, the due process clause, since it might be broadly interpreted in the light of usage and legal history, has been supplemented by several limiting provisions. This means that, whether such practices are due process or not, the United States may not resort to them.

I turn now to the other amendments. The First provides: "*Congress shall make no law* respecting an establishment of religion, or prohibiting the free exercise thereof; or abridging the freedom of speech, or of the press; or the right of the people peaceably to assemble, and to petition the Government for a redress of grievances." When this amendment was adopted, the law of libel was well understood. Criminal punishment and civil redress were open for any abuse of the right to print and publish. Criminal sanction might be imposed under existing law for riots and breaches of the peace due to abuse of free speech. The people of this country were familiar with what had been enacted and enforced in Great Britain. They were familiar with the fact that licensing acts had been passed which were used for the suppression of free expression of opinion.[21] All the amendment purports to do is to forbid statutory enactments intended prospectively to limit free speech—to impose previous restraints on publication.

If, in the view of the proponents of the First Amendment, the due process clause of the Fifth Amendment already precluded the passage of any such laws as are mentioned in the First, it was mere repetition to adopt both. The due process clause of the Fourteenth Amendment has not been construed as if it provided "no State shall *make any law* abridging the freedom of speech or of the press." On the contrary, it is settled doctrine that a state may act in violation of the federal Constitution either by its legislature, by its executive,[22] or by its courts.[23] Action by any of these is denominated "state action" when a question under the amendment is mooted in the Supreme Court. Thus, by the sweeping expansion of the guaranty of due process to embrace the so-called liberties of the First Amendment, the states seem to be placed under a more rigorous control by application of the concept of due process than that which was intended to bind the United States under the First Amendment. So it seems the Fourteenth now not only embodies the prohibition of the First against previous restraints, but employs a concept of liberty held to be a corollary of the First.

Let us proceed with an examination of the other amendments. The Second was obviously intended to protect the state militia forces against deprivation of their arms by the United States. The Third forbade the quartering of soldiers in homes in time of peace and also in time of war, except under a law to be enacted in the premises. Both these amendments can only by a stretch of interpretation be held to be embraced within the guaranty of due process; obviously, such was not the thought of those who drafted them. They

[21] See Near v. Minnesota, 283 U.S. 697, at p. 713 (1931).
[22] Sterling v. Constantin, 287 U.S. 378 (1932).
[23] Bridges v. California, 309 U.S. 649 (1940).

evidently did not believe they were superfluous or tautological with the due process clause of the Fifth.

The language of the Fourth Amendment reinforces the view that the due process clause of the Fifth was intended only to protect those liberties which had traditionally been protected in England and observed in the Colonies. The provisions against unreasonable searches and seizures and requiring warrants to issue only on oath and on probable cause were obviously intended to supplement the due process clause, for, in English history, there had been practices contrary to those banned by the Fourth Amendment.

Again, the guaranties of the Sixth Amendment that one accused of crime shall be afforded speedy public trial by an impartial jury in the state and district where the crime was committed, that he shall have the right to be informed of the nature and cause of accusation, to be confronted by the witnesses against him, to have compulsory process for obtaining witnesses in his favor, and the assistance of counsel, are all precautionary provisions, added or subtracted, as the case may be, from the traditional concept of due process of law embodied in the Fifth Amendment. And finally, the Seventh and Eighth Amendments, which provide for a jury trial in certain actions at common law, forbid excessive bail, excessive fines, and cruel and unusual punishments, were wholly unnecessary if, in fact, these rights were embraced in the concept of due process. So all the additional guaranties embodied in the first eight amendments, if they are embraced in the due process clause of the Fifth, were wholly unnecessary. If the converse is true and it was necessary to specify these matters as against action by the federal government, notwithstanding the due process clause, it should have been equally necessary to spell these matters out in the Fourteenth as prohibitions directed to state action.

Except for the liberties named in the First, and the just

compensation clause of the Fifth, the Court has repeatedly voiced this view. The following have been the conclusions. The due process clause does not require a state to proceed by indictment in charging a serious crime,[24] though the Fifth so requires the United States; a state may provide for a verdict by less than twelve jurors[25] and may abolish jury trials in civil cases.[26] The clause of the Fifth Amendment against compelling an individual to be a witness against himself does not apply to the states.[27] The requirement of the Sixth Amendment which gives an accused the right to counsel in all cases in federal courts[28] does not apply to state court trials, and due process does not require appointment of counsel in all cases.[29] The prohibition of double jeopardy of the Fifth Amendment has no application to state action.[30] The prosecutor may read the deposition of a witness whose presence at a state criminal trial cannot be procured.[31] On the other hand, it has been held that the due process clause requires a state court to appoint counsel for an ignorant and impecunious defendant charged with a serious crime;[32] and recently it has been adjudged that due process guarantees against unreasonable searches and seizures, notwithstanding the fact that these are separately dealt with by the Fourth Amendment,[33] although the *majority* of the Court in this latest case violently denied that the result was due to any ab-

[24] Hurtado v. California, 110 U.S. 516 (1884); Gaines v. Washington, 277 U.S. 81, 86 (1928).

[25] Jordan v. Massachusetts, 225 U.S. 167, 176 (1912).

[26] Frank v. Mangum, 237 U.S. 309, 341 (1915); Hawkins v. Bleakly, 243 U.S. 210, 216 (1917).

[27] Twining v. New Jersey, 211 U.S. 78 (1908); Adamson v. California, 332 U.S. 46 (1947).

[28] Johnson v. Zerbst, 304 U.S. 458 (1938).

[29] Betts v. Brady, 316 U.S. 455 (1942); Bute v. Illinois, 333 U.S. 640 (1948).

[30] Palko v. Connecticut, 302 U.S. 319 (1937).

[31] West v. Louisiana, 194 U.S. 258 (1904).

[32] Powell v. Alabama, 287 U.S. 45 (1932); Gibbs v. Burke, 337 U.S. 773 (1949).

[33] Wolf v. Colorado, *supra*, note 19.

sorption of the Fourth Amendment by the due process clause of the Fourteenth.

In this course of decision, the Court has adopted at various times contradictory reasoning. In *Hurtado* v. *California*,[34] it was at pains to show that the due process clause of the Fourteenth Amendment did not require an indictment in the charging of serious offenses because that matter had been covered in a separate clause of the Fifth Amendment, and it was obvious that the first eight amendments should not be construed so that any clause in any one of them was superfluous or tautological. Some years later in *Powell* v. *Alabama*,[35] the Court freely admitted that if "due process" means what is traditional practice at common law and in our colonial practice, the right to counsel in felony cases does not fall within it. The Court pointed out that some of the colonies recognized the right in their own courts and hence, as a matter of precaution, the Sixth Amendment made the same guaranty as respects federal prosecutions. In its discussion of the concept of due process, the Court stated that while customary practice in England is an aid to construction, it is not conclusive. In *Snyder* v. *Massachusetts*,[36] although it was shown that, by constitution and statute dating from the earliest times, practically every state had recognized as fundamental to a fair trial the right of a defendant in a criminal case to be present throughout the entire trial, from empanelling of jury until verdict, the Court held this fact did not mean that the exercise of the right so recognized was essential to due process. In *Palko* v. *Connecticut*,[37] the Court rejected the contention that the prohibition of double jeopardy contained in the Fifth Amendment was embraced in the concept of due process under the Fourteenth.

Despite all this, in the very recent case of *Wolf* v. *Colo-*

[34] *Supra*, note 24.
[35] *Supra*, note 32; pp. 60–61.
[36] 291 U.S. 97 (1934).
[37] 302 U.S. 319 (1937).

rado,[38] a majority of the Court has reversed a position long-held and has now pronounced unreasonable searches and seizures by state officers a violation of the due process guaranteed by the Fourteenth Amendment. I shall have more to say presently concerning the possible remedy for violation of the amendment. However, the test of a violation of due process laid down in this recent decision is of importance. The due process clause is said to exact from the states all that is "implicit in the concept of ordered liberty." It is further said that the concept is a living one, that it guarantees basic rights, not because they have become petrified as of any one time, but because due process follows the advancing standards of a free society as to what is deemed reasonable and right. It is to be applied, according to this view, to facts and circumstances as they arise, the cases falling on one side of the line or the other as a majority of nine justices appraise conduct as either implicit in the concept of ordered liberty or as lying without the confines of that vague concept. Of course, in this view, the due process clause of the Fifth Amendment, which confessedly must be construed like that of the Fourteenth, may be repetitious of many of the other guaranties of the first eight amendments and may render many of their provisions superfluous.

So construed, the due process clause places in the Supreme Court an enormous power[39] over the legislation of the states and the procedures of their courts, as well as the powers of their executives.[40] I believe that whether this be thought wise or unwise, statesmanlike or the reverse, it is contrary to the views of those who adopted the Constitution, and that even such a sweeping enactment as the Fourteenth Amendment

[38] *Supra*, note 19.

[39] See the dissenting opinion of Mr. Justice Black in Adamson v. California, 332 U.S. 46, 68 (1947).

[40] Sterling v. Constantin, 287 U.S. 378 (1932); compare Moyer v. Peabody, 212 U.S. 78 (1909).

was not intended to put the states in tutelage to the Supreme Court in any such fashion.

It is now of interest to examine how this vast power has been exercised by the Court. Let us examine one or two fields of adjudication. Since *Powell* v. *Alabama*,[41] the Court has repeatedly held that the right to counsel for preparation and trial in a serious criminal case is a requirement of due process; that no waiver of the right is lightly to be implied; and that the right extends even to one who apparently voluntarily pleaded guilty, if there is any question of his competence so to do.[42] It is true that the Court has attempted to leave some discretion in the state courts as to whether a defendant shall have counsel. In *Betts* v. *Brady*,[43] it was held that where it does not appear that the defendant needed counsel, and where it is shown that the state courts have not, except in serious cases and those in which it appears the defendant requires the aid of counsel, been accustomed to appoint counsel for him, a refusal or neglect to appoint is not a denial of due process. This holding was based on the theory that, notwithstanding the provisions of the Sixth Amendment, the right to have counsel in every case is not an element of due process. This view, however, has been severely criticized by several members of the Court, who would hold the requirement of the Sixth Amendment is taken over by the Fourteenth, or that due process requires the appointment.

Another field in which the due process clause has been the subject of much dispute is that of enforced confession.

[41] *Supra*, note 32.

[42] Avery v. Alabama, 308 U.S. 444 (1940); Walker v. Johnston, 312 U.S. 275 (1941); Smith v. O'Grady, 312 U.S. 329 (1941); Glasser v. United States, 315 U.S. 60 (1942); Williams v. Kaiser, 323 U.S. 471 (1945); Tomkins v. Missouri, 323 U.S. 485 (1945); House v. Mayo, 324 U.S. 42 (1945); White v. Ragen, 324 U.S. 760 (1945); Rice v. Olson, 324 U.S. 786 (1945); Hawk v. Olson, 326 U.S. 271 (1945); Carter v. Illinois, 329 U.S. 173 (1946); DeMeerleer v. Michigan, 329 U.S. 663 (1947); compare Canizio v. New York, 327 U.S. 82 (1946), and Foster v. Illinois, 332 U.S. 134 (1947).

[43] 316 U.S. 455 (1942).

In a number of cases it was held that the evidence showed a confession to have been obtained by coercion, either mental or physical, and that it was therefore involuntary, though the judges and a jury in the state court had concurred in the view that the confession was voluntary.[44] Thus far the Court has reserved to itself the right to determine on all the facts whether the confession was in truth voluntary and has held a confession voluntary although the result of illegal conduct on the part of state officers.[45]

It would seem that the use which may be made of a confession should be governed by the same test under the Fifth Amendment as against the United States and under the Fourteenth as against a state, but this has not been so. In *McNabb v. United States*,[46] the Court found that the detention of the prisoner without his being taken before a committing magistrate was a violation of statute law and held that incriminating statements made by him while he was thus illegally detained were inadmissible in his trial. No decision was made as to the voluntary character of his statements. It was enough that they had been made while he was illegally confined. The Court used certain phrases to characterize the conduct of the federal officers which I cannot distinguish from statements used in characterizing the admission by state courts of coerced confessions as violating due process.

The case was, therefore, not decided on constitutional grounds. On the contrary, it was held that the supervisory power of the Supreme Court over criminal trials gave it authority to order the exclusion of evidence obtained during

---

[44] Brown v. Mississippi, 297 U.S. 278 (1936); Chambers v. Florida, 309 U.S. 227 (1940); White v. Texas, 310 U.S. 530 (1940); Ashcraft v. Tennessee, 322 U.S. 143 (1944); Haley v. Ohio, 332 U.S. 596 (1948); Watts v. Indiana, 338 U.S. 49 (1949); Turner v. Pennsylvania, 338 U.S. 62 (1949); Harris v. South Carolina, 338 U.S. 68 (1949).

[45] Lisenba v. California, 314 U.S. 219 (1941); Lyons v. Oklahoma, 322 U.S. 596 (1944).

[46] 318 U.S. 332 (1943).

the course of violation of statutes which expressed the policy of Congress with respect to the arrest and holding of persons accused of crime. The decision seems to me to hold that, so long as the policy of Congress prohibits certain acts, the Court may, in its discretion, exclude evidence obtained where the violations of such policy occur. The evidentiary value of the confession as voluntary or the reverse is immaterial.

In the same volume of the *Reports* which contains the *Mc-Nabb* case, there appears the case of *Anderson* v. *United States*,[47] in which conduct of state officers, in violation of a state statute, was held to poison a confession made to federal officers while the prisoner was under illegal detention, so that the confession was inadmissible in a federal prosecution. On the other hand, in *United States* v. *Mitchell*,[48] it was held that an admission of guilt made immediately upon the prisoner's arrest and before a period of illegal detention was a voluntary confession, and that the policy against admission of confessions made while the prisoner was illegally held had no application to the case. In *Upshaw* v. *United States*,[49] the prisoner was arrested on suspicion and without a warrant. He was held in custody some thirty hours and questioned without being taken before a committing magistrate. The police officers stated that the reason they so held him was because they were uncertain of his guilt. Following the *McNabb* case, the Court decided that to hold a man on suspicion, without a hearing and commitment, was a violation of federal law and that any confession made during the period of such illegal detention was inadmissible in evidence against him. In *Weeks* v. *United States*,[50] federal officers had violated the Fourth Amendment in seizing papers belonging to the defendant. The Court held that the papers so seized were inadmissible in evidence. In *Silverthorne Lumber Co.* v.

[47] 318 U.S. 350 (1943).
[48] 322 U.S. 65 (1944).
[49] 335 U.S. 410 (1948).
[50] 232 U.S. 383 (1914).

United States,[51] federal officers stole papers of a defendant without a warrant, copied them, returned them to the defendant, and then by subpoena required their production at the trial of the case. It was held that they were inadmissible.

This being the state of the law, the Court took the case of *Wolf* v. *Colorado*,[52] in which state officers conducted a search and seizure which would have violated the Fourth Amendment had they been federal officers. The state court admitted the evidence obtained. By a sharply divided Court, the Supreme Court affirmed a conviction. I have already adverted to the fact that, whereas the Court had repeatedly held that the due process clause of the Fourteenth Amendment did not draw to it the provisions of the Fourth, it nevertheless here denounces unreasonable searches and seizures as a violation of the due process clause of the Fourteenth. If it were to apply the same rule of exclusion which it has applied in federal prosecutions, in the case of papers seized in violation of the Fourth Amendment, it should here have held that the matters seized were inadmissible in evidence. On the contrary, it holds that whether these shall be admitted is not a matter of due process, but a matter of state policy as to trial, which rests solely within the competence of state courts; that the admission or exclusion of evidence is not a matter of due process, but a state question beyond the reach of the Fourteenth Amendment. If this is so, then what becomes of the decisions requiring the exclusion from evidence of confessions obtained by violations of rights guaranteed by the due process clause? The violation of due process consists in the admission of the coerced confession. The ruling on the admissibility of the confession is a ruling as to the result which ought to follow from the violation of the prisoner's constitutional right. If a violation of his rights in the seizure of his papers does not vitiate their evidentiary value, it is

[51] 251 U.S. 385 (1920).   [52] 338 U.S. 25 (1949).

difficult to see why a violation of his right not to be coerced into incriminating himself ought to be held to vitiate his confession, as has consistently been held. It is suggested in the *Wolf* case that the state may criminally punish the violation of right, or may award civil damages in a trespass action, or, presumably, leave the offender to go unpunished and free of civil liability.

In the *Wolf* case, a minority of the Court dissented on the ground that the only adequate redress for the violation of the defendant's rights was the exclusion of the improperly seized evidence. And I think they made a pretty convincing case. But, I submit, the whole discussion of the admissibility of the evidence misses the constitutional question involved. It assumes that the violation of due process is the forbidden seizure. If the Fourth Amendment does not forbid the conduct of the state officers, then the majority correctly held that the illegality of their conduct and any punishment they should suffer for it were pure questions of state law, with which the Supreme Court has nothing to do. But the due process question, if any, in the case was the use of the material in the trial to convict the defendant.

This has always been the basis of the reversal of state convictions obtained by the use in the trial of coerced confessions. The state may or may not punish its officers for infringing the law in dealing with a prisoner. Surely they can be held both civilly and criminally liable under state law for resorting to torture of a prisoner to compel him to confess, for holding him incommunicado, for denying him opportunity to get counsel, and so forth. Assume that they do all these things and obtain a confession, but do not use the confession at his trial or for discovering other evidence against him. Would the Supreme Court set aside his conviction in such a case? Would it hold that a federal court could, or a state court must, punish the officers because, forsooth, their illegal and criminal acts were a denial of due process? To ask the question is to answer it. Violations of state law by individuals can never be state action, despite rulings to the contrary.

The use of a coerced confession in the defendant's trial is, however, another matter. The whole course of our legal history forbids that the fruits of the rack and the thumbscrew be used in a court of law as the materials of conviction.

Thus in *Brown* v. *Mississippi*[53] it was said: "The rack and the torture chamber may not be substituted for the witness stand. . . . Nor may a state through the action of its officers *contrive a conviction through the pretense of a trial* . . . and the trial . . . is a mere pretense where the state authorities have contrived a conviction resting solely upon confessions obtained by violence. . . . It would be difficult to conceive of methods more revolting to the sense of justice than those taken to procure the confessions of the petitioners, and the use of the confessions *thus obtained as the basis for conviction and sentence was a clear denial of due process*."

And in *Lisenba* v. *California*:[54] "Such unfairness exists when a coerced confession is used as a means of obtaining a verdict of guilt."

This is why judgments of conviction where coerced confessions were used have been reversed by the Supreme Court time and again. If the Constitution forbids coercing confessions, then under the ruling in the *Wolf* case it equally forbids unreasonable searches and seizures. It is because, and only because, it so forbids that under the traditional requirement of fairness in a trial the use of the fruits of the forbidden practices are inadmissible as proof of guilt. Notwithstanding the *Wolf* decision, the Court, at the same term, adhered to the

[53] 297 U.S. 278, 286 (1936). My italics in the quotation.
[54] 314 U.S. 219, 236–237 (1941).

doctrine that the use of a coerced confession voided a conviction in a state court.[55]

What sort of rule is it that imposes one consequence for one violation of the due process clause and another consequence for a different violation? Does the result depend upon the question whether the violation is big or little? Do some violations require one result and others a different one?

The truth seems to be that the division in the Court as to whether the due process clause embodies the first eight amendments is modifying the attitude of a majority of the justices. There are two cases in point. In *Louisiana* v. *Resweber*,[56] the appellee contended that the provisions of the Fifth and Eighth Amendments prohibited the state from making a second attempt to electrocute him, pursuant to a sentence of death, the first having failed. He claimed the proposed attempt would subject him to double jeopardy and to cruel and unusual punishment. Four justices of the Supreme Court held that such a second attempt would violate due process. Five justices joined in the opinion which disposed of the case in this fashion: "We shall examine the circumstances under the assumption, but without deciding, that violations of the principles of the Fifth and Eighth Amendments as to double jeopardy and cruel and unusual punishment, would be violative of the due process clause of the Fourteenth Amendment." Mr. Justice Black was of the majority. It is evident that unless the majority of the Court had "assumed" these propositions the case could not have been decided. We are led to speculate when the Court will hold that the Fourteenth has absorbed the Fifth and Eighth Amendments.

In *Wolf* v. *Colorado*,[57] Mr. Justice Frankfurter, the most

[55] Watts v. Indiana, 338 U.S. 49 (1949); Turner v. Pennsylvania, 338 U.S. 62 (1949); Harris v. South Carolina, 338 U.S. 68 (1949).
[56] 329 U.S. 459 (1947).
[57] *Supra*, note 19.

ardent protagonist of the doctrine that the Fourteenth Amendment reënacted none of the early amendments, in order to make up a majority for the Court's decision had to concede that an unreasonable search or seizure, by state officers, though not a violation of the Fourth Amendment, because that amendment was not binding on a state, was nevertheless a violation of due process. Thus the Fourth Amendment, like the First and portions of the Fifth, has come in against state action by the back door as a corollary of due process. I suspect that, as in the *Resweber* case, this concession was necessary to get a majority of the Court.

It is within the possibilities that soon the Court will adopt the view of the present minority that due process is, as Mr. Justice Frankfurter has phrased it, shorthand for the text of the first eight amendments. In order to hold his position against this view, he has had to extend the concept of due process and, at the same time, abandon the logical result of that extension. While adhering to the view that the Fourth Amendment, as such, does not apply to state action, he has had to abandon a doctrine long held by the Court. Until the *Wolf* case was decided, the Court held—as a corollary of the doctrine that the Fourth Amendment did not affect state action—that searches and seizures by state officers, which, if made by federal officers, would have been illegal and would have required the exclusion from evidence of the seized material, did not require federal courts to exclude it. Thus in *Byars* v. *United States*[58] it was said: "We do not question the right of the federal government to avail itself of evidence improperly seized by state officers operating entirely on their own account." Other Supreme Court cases[59] and a body of lower court decisions are to the same effect.

---

[58] 273 U.S. 28, 33 (1927).

[59] Weeks v. United States, 232 U.S. 383 (1914); Burdeau v. McDowell, 256 U.S. 465 (1921); Center v. United States, 267 U.S. 575 (1925).

The *Wolf* case definitely holds that the seizure there in question was a violation of federal constitutional rights. What matter whose agent committed it? In *Gambino* v. *United States*,[60] a federal officer was concerned in the seizure with state officers, but what Mr. Justice Brandeis said for the Court seems equally applicable in the *Wolf* case, now that the Court has characterized what the state officers did as a violation of due process, The opinion reads: "But as the conviction of these defendants rests wholly upon evidence obtained by invasion of their constitutional rights, we are of opinion that the judgment should be reversed."

It would seem that we have a strange medley of federal and state law. Sometimes a violation of due process by a state leads to a reversal of a judgment of conviction; sometimes it does not. We are not told what is the distinction.

Many actions which are not a denial of due process have the effect of rendering relevant evidence inadmissible in the federal courts; not so in state courts. There is a federal judicial policy which condemns certain acts which fall short of a denial of constitutional rights. What are they? Future decisions may inform us. Now, in addition to being the final arbiter of the limits of due process, the Court has become the final arbiter concerning an undefined bundle of other rights of lower order.

We can think of many difficulties this situation creates. Wire tapping is "dirty business." It seems not to be a violation of any provision of the Constitution, unless of the due process clause. The Court avoided a decision in *Nardone* v. *United States*[61] by finding a Congressional statutory policy against wire tapping. Suppose it had not been able to do so. Whether a denial of due process or not, what about the admissibility of the wire taps in a state court or in a federal court? Entrapment is also a dirty business. What is to be its effect in the

[60] 275 U.S. 310, 319 (1927).   [61] 302 U.S. 379 (1937).

trial of one entrapped in state or federal courts? Many other instances might be cited.

One further matter needs mention. Section 5 of the Fourteenth Amendment provides: "The Congress shall have power to enforce by appropriate legislation the provisions of this Article." In the other two amendments adopted as a result of the Civil War, Congress introduced this innovation: both the Thirteenth and Fifteenth contain a section giving Congress authority to enforce the provisions of each of them by legislation.

In the reconstruction era, Congress passed so-called Civil Rights Bills under the power so conferred. Resort to suit or prosecution under this legislation has been infrequent and, until recently, has raised no serious questions. But now, it seems, there is likely to be more general reliance on these acts. This raises serious questions of the division of powers.

It must be conceded that by the ratification of the three Civil War amendments the people expressly gave Congress an authority over the individual citizen, which, if it existed, was only implied from other provisions of the Constitution. It must also be admitted that if Congress stays within the fair intendment of the language of the amendments, its legislation is valid.

What is the scope of the powers so conferred? Pursuant to the grant of power, Congress has adopted several statutes. One is the Act of March 1, 1875, later 8 United States Code, Section 44, and now Section 243 of Title 18 of the United States Code. That law provided: "No citizen possessing all other qualifications which are or may be prescribed by law shall be disqualified for service as grand or petit juror in any court of the United States, or of any state, on account of race, color, or previous condition of servitude." In *Ex parte Virginia*,[62] the Supreme Court sustained the act against a

[62] 100 U.S. 339 (1880).

petition in habeas corpus by a Virginia judge who had been arrested and indicted in a federal court for violation of the provisions of the statute in the drawing of a jury. The Court said:

"All of the amendments derive much of their force from this latter provision. It is not said the *judicial power* of the general government shall extend to enforcing the prohibitions and protecting the rights and immunities guaranteed. It is not said that branch of the government shall be authorized to declare void any action of a State in violation of the prohibitions. It is the power of Congress which has been enlarged. Congress is authorized to *enforce* the prohibitions by appropriate legislation. Some legislation is contemplated to make the amendments fully effective. Whatever legislation is appropriate, that is, adapted to carry out the objects the amendments have in view, whatever tends to enforce submission to the prohibitions they contain, and to secure to all persons the enjoyment of perfect equality of civil rights and the equal protection of the laws against State denial or invasion, if not prohibited, is brought within the domain of congressional power."[63]

At the same time the Court decided two cases, *Strauder* v. *West Virginia* and *Virginia* v. *Rives*,[64] in which it held that discrimination in the matter of race or color in the drawing of a state grand jury was a violation of the equal protection clause of the Fourteenth Amendment—this without reference to any statutory definition by Congress.

In *Fay* v. *New York*,[65] the civil rights statute in question is quoted and the Court says:

"For us the majestic generalities of the Fourteenth Amendment are thus reduced to a concrete statutory command

[63] Pages 345–346.　　　　　　　[65] 332 U.S. 261, 282 (1947).
[64] 100 U.S. 303 (1880); 100 U.S. 313 (1880).

when cases involve race or color which is wanting in every other case of alleged discrimination. This statute was a factor so decisive in establishing the Negro case precedents that the Court even hinted that there might be no judicial power to intervene except in matters authorized by Acts of Congress."

The opinion proceeds, however, "We do not mean that no case of discrimination in jury drawing except those involving race or color can carry such unjust consequences as to amount to a denial of equal protection or due process of law." The Court adds that, since Congress has dealt with the jury matter, any interference by a court outside the limits prescribed in the statute would require a very strong showing.

In 1871 Congress adopted a civil rights bill[66] which provides for suits against "any person who under the color of any law, statute, ordinance, regulation, custom, or usage, of any State . . . subjects, or causes to be subjected, any citizen of the United States or other person . . . to the deprivation of any rights, privileges or immunities described by the Constitution."

In *Hague* v. *C.I.O,*[67] a suit for injunction was brought in a federal district court against certain officials who claimed to be enforcing local ordinances. Their acts were attacked as violations of the right of freedom of speech and assembly, and hence a violation of due process as defined in the Fourteenth Amendment by reference to the liberties ascribed to the prohibitions of the First Amendment. Four justices, for whom Mr. Justice Stone spoke, found that jurisdiction of such a case, notwithstanding that no specific amount was in controversy, had been conferred by the Judiciary Act, and then went on to determine whether the suit could be maintained under the civil rights statute. Mr. Justice Stone was

[66] Now Title 8, Section 43, U.S. Code.
[67] 307 U.S. 496 (1939).

careful to point out that the conduct charged constituted violations of due process as defined in prior decisions of the Supreme Court, and, therefore, the case fell clearly within the statute.

Section 20 of the Criminal Code of the United States[68] provides that "whoever, under color of any law, statute, ordinance, regulation, or custom, wilfully subjects, or causes to be subjected, any inhabitant of any state . . . to the deprivation of any rights, privileges, or immunities secured or protected by the Constitution and laws of the United States" shall be guilty of a crime.

In *Screws* v. *United States*,[69] an indictment was found in a federal district court against peace officers of the State of Georgia, charging that they had willfully caused one Hall to be deprived of rights, privileges, or immunities secured to him by the Fourteenth Amendment, and specifying these as the right not to be deprived of life without due process of law and the right to be tried upon a charge on which he had been arrested by due process of law and, if found guilty, to be punished in accordance with the state laws. The indictment charged that, by assaulting and beating Hall, these officers had caused his death and so deprived him of the recited constitutional rights. The case was tried and the jury found a verdict of guilty. The Supreme Court reversed and remanded the decision, by vote of a majority of the justices, for error in the trial judge's charge to the jury, because he had not pointed out that the defendants could only be guilty if they had willfully, that is, intentionally, violated the provisions of the Constitution securing due process of law. Three justices dissented on several grounds, which may thus be summarized: First, that Congress did not intend to make violation of the laws of a state (which the conduct of the defendants undoubtedly was) also a violation of the Fourteenth Amend-

[68] 18 U.S.C., § 52.   [69] 325 U.S. 91 (1945).

ment. Next, that the federal courts ought not, where a serious crime has been committed punishable by heavy penalty under state law, entertain jurisdiction under a federal statute imposing a comparatively mild penalty. Next, that it could hardly be said that what was done was done under color of state law when the very acts committed were obviously serious crimes under that law. And, lastly, that when due process is necessarily so vague a concept that its contours can be marked out only in individual cases after the fullest consideration of all the facts, to hold that a state official may be indicted for violation of due process is to hold him to so vague a standard of conduct as to make the statute, if so construed, unconstitutional.

In *Wolf* v. *Colorado*,[70] where the Court held that an unreasonable search or seizure constituted a violation of due process, Mr. Justice Frankfurter said:

"And though we have interpreted the Fourth Amendment to forbid the admission of such evidence [in Federal Courts], a different question would be presented if Congress under its legislative powers were to pass a statute purporting to undo the *Weeks* doctrine. We would then be faced with the problem of the respect to be accorded the legislative judgment on an issue as to which, in default of that judgment, we have been forced to depend upon our own. Problems of a converse character, also not before us, would be presented should Congress under Section 5 of the Fourteenth Amendment undertake to enforce the rights there guaranteed by attempting to make the *Weeks* doctrine binding upon the States."

I have cited these cases dealing with enforcement statutes with the purpose of showing that the power of Congress under Section 5 of the Fourteenth Amendment to enforce

[70] 338 U.S. 25, 33 (1949).

its provisions by legislation has created a situation that is far from clear. Is it a corollary of the power to enforce that Congress also possesses the power to define what are violations of due process? If so, and to whatever extent it may be so, final interpretation of the Constitution is not in the Supreme Court but in Congress. Perhaps this is the reason for the reservation made by Mr. Justice Jackson which I have mentioned. Suppose that Congress should essay to make it a crime for a state court to admit or not to admit certain evidence, on the theory that the proscribed court action would be a violation of due process. I cannot believe that the Supreme Court would not be bound to examine and pass upon the validity of the judgment of Congress so embodied in legislation. Doubtless, as in other cases, deference would be paid to the judgment of the legislature, but if that deference is to be carried far, it may well result that, with changing notions of policy, the limits of due process may remain to be fixed and settled by the legislature rather than by the judiciary.

In summary, I think it fair to say that, progressively, the Supreme Court has limited and surrendered the role the Constitution was intended to confer on it. *Vox populi, vox Dei* was not the theory on which the charter was drawn. The sharp division of powers intended has become blurred. Perhaps this was inevitable. Perhaps it is a beneficial development. However that may be, it seems obvious that doctrines announced as corollaries to express grants of power to the Congress have more and more circumscribed the pristine powers of the states, which were intended to be reserved to them by the Constitution, and that resistance to the expansion of those doctrines seems to have weakened as our nation has grown.

Table of Cases

70
71

72
74
75
76
77
79
81
83
85
88